Palgrave Studies in Cyberpsychology

Series Editor
Jens Binder
Nottingham Trent University
Nottingham, UK

Studies in Cyberpsychology aims to foster and to chart the scope of research driven by a psychological understanding of the effects of the 'new technology' that is shaping our world after the digital revolution. The series takes an inclusive approach and considers all aspects of human behaviours and experiential states in relation to digital technologies, to the Internet, and to virtual environments. As such, Cyberpsychology reaches out to several neighbouring disciplines, from Human-Computer Interaction to Media and Communication Studies. A core question underpinning the series concerns the actual psychological novelty of new technology. To what extent do we need to expand conventional theories and models to account for cyberpsychological phenomena? At which points is the ubiquitous digitisation of our everyday lives shifting the focus of research questions and research needs? Where do we see implications for our psychological functioning that are likely to outlast shortlived fashions in technology use?

More information about this series at
http://www.springer.com/series/14636

Lucy R. Betts

Cyberbullying

Approaches, Consequences and Interventions

Lucy R. Betts
Nottingham Trent University
Nottingham, United Kingdom

Palgrave Studies in Cyberpsychology
ISBN 978-1-137-50008-3   ISBN 978-1-137-50009-0   (eBook)
DOI 10.1057/978-1-137-50009-0

Library of Congress Control Number: 2016942659

Cover illustration: Abstract Bricks and Shadows © Stephen Bonk/Fotolia.co.uk

Printed on acid-free paper

This Palgrave Macmillan imprint is published by Springer Nature
The registered company is Macmillan Publishers Ltd. London

ACKNOWLEDGEMENTS

With thanks to my family and friends for their constant support.

CONTENTS

CONTENTS

LIST OF TABLES

CHAPTER 1

Introduction

Abstract Digital technology has permeated many aspects of our day-to-day activities, with many organisations becoming 'digital by default'. With this increased connectivity and digital technology use come many benefits; however, these benefits are often offset by more adverse consequences. Since 2003, one consequence that has rapidly increased in prominence in the research literature and the media is cyberbullying. This chapter will provide readers with a brief outline of cyberbullying and then an introduction to the remainder of the book.

Keywords Digital technology • Cyberbullying • Cyber bullycide

Digital technology has afforded us many benefits and has enabled users to complete many day-to-day activities in a more efficient and effective manner. Cyberspace provides young people with a place of positive discourse and a positive nurturing environment where behaviour can promote social responsibility and encourage caring and respect (Cassidy, Jackson, & Brown, 2009). Young people also regard the Internet as a 'safe' space where they can express themselves (Davis, Ambrose, & Orond, 2014). However, despite these benefits, researchers have argued that one of the unintended consequences of digital technology is cyberbullying (Tokunaga, 2010). This chapter will begin by providing a general overview of aggression,

© The Editor(s) (if applicable) and The Author(s) 2016   1
L.R. Betts, *Cyberbullying*, DOI 10.1057/978-1-137-50009-0_1

harassment, and bullying and then move to discussing a brief background to cyberbullying before presenting an overview of the rest of this book.

1.1   AGGRESSION, HARASSMENT, AND BULLYING

The term 'aggressive behaviour' is used by researchers to describe any behaviour that is intended to cause harm, which can include physical, verbal, and psychological (Liu, Lewis, & Evans, 2013). According to Liu et al., aggressive behaviour is distinct from violence because although violence typically involves physical behaviour, aggression does not. Aggressive behaviours have also been classified according to whether they are proactive or reactive. Proactive aggression, also known as instrumental aggression, relates to behaviours that are deliberate and are motivated by the desire to achieve a particular goal (Card & Little, 2006). Reactive aggression, also known as defensive aggression, describes behaviours that are motivated in response to a perceived offence, frustration, or anger, or are emotionally dysregulated (Card & Little, 2006). Additionally, aggressive behaviour can be regarded as direct or indirect. Direct aggression involves verbal and physical acts aimed at the target, whereas indirect aggression involves acts intended to cause harm to the target by using others such as gossip, rumours, and exclusion from social situations (Archer & Coyne, 2005). A number of studies have reported the link between aggression and bullying (e.g., Lee, 2009; Roland, & Idsøe, 2001) and aggression and cyberbullying (e.g., Ang, Huan, & Florell, 2014; Orue & Andershed, 2015).

Harassment is a form of aggressive behaviour that is linked to bullying and cyberbullying. In the workplace, harassment has been conceptualised as negative interactions which are designed to harm the target (Neall & Tuckey, 2014). Behaviours can include incivility, obscene gestures, dirty looks, threats, verbal attacks, belittling, and purposefully ignoring someone (Bowling & Beehr, 2006). Experiencing work-based harassment has been found to negatively impact on the targets' psychological and physical well-being (Raver & Nishii, 2010). Harassment can take many other forms such as sociodemographic, sexual, or based on appearance, race, ethnicity, and weight and, for young people, experiences of harassment often co-occur (Bucchianeri, Eisenberg, & Neumark-Sztainer, 2013). Experiencing harassment in face-to-face settings is also associated with experiencing harassment when using technology (Beran, Rinaldi, Bickham, & Rich, 2012).

1.2 BRIEF OUTLINE OF CYBERBULLYING

The term 'cyberbullying' first started to appear in the academic literature in 2003 following the launch of a website by Bill Belsey (http://www.cyberbullying.ca/) that addressed cyberbullying in Canada (Bauman & Bellmore, 2015); since then, the number of studies examining cyberbullying has increased exponentially. Through examining academic databases, Zych, Ortega-Ruiz, and Del Rey (2015) quantified the increase in academic articles from 2003 to the present day. Between 2001 and 2005, 4 articles on the topic of cyberbullying were identified; however, this figure rose to 42 between 2006 and 2010. After 2011, the authors identified a further 30 articles in the area of cyberbullying. A recent search of Google scholar, undertaken on 6 January 2016, yielded over 27,000 hits for the term cyberbullying. This figure compares with the 5280 hits when the search was limited to 2014 and 4650 hits in 2015. Together, these figures not only reflect the rate of growth in the academic community exploring cyberbullying but also likely reflect society's growing concern about this topic.

Researchers', educational practitioners', and parents' interest in cyberbullying can be attributed to the many consequences associated with involvement in face-to-face bullying and cyberbullying (which are outlined in Chap. 5). However, perhaps the greatest catalyst for society's interest in cyberbullying is the many well-documented cases of 'cyber bullycide'. Cyber bullycide is the term used to describe a case where a young person has committed suicide, and one of the causes of their actions is attributed to cyberbullying and negative experiences in the digital world, for example, the case of Phoebe Prince who was 15 years old when she committed suicide after receiving threats through instant messenger and social networking sites (Moreno, 2011). The term cyberbullying has also permeated everyday language; a recent example is the TED talk given by Monica Lewinsky in March 2015 where she states that she was 'patient zero of losing a personal reputation on a global scale almost instantaneously'. (http://www.ted.com/talks/monica_lewinsky_the_price_of_shame#t-573959). Lewinsky goes on to argue that the global media coverage, facilitated by the Internet, she experienced in 1998 was unprecedented harassment that today would have been recognised as cyberbullying.

1.3   Overview of the Text

Compared to other forms of bullying, cyberbullying is a relatively new phenomenon that reflects, in part, how digital technology has permeated day-to-day-life. Given the relative 'newness' of this phenomenon, there is considerable ambiguity and debate within the research literature: This book will focus on some of these key issues and current debates.

Chapter 2 presents an overview of the issues surrounding the definition of cyberbullying. The term cyberbullying can be regarded as an 'umbrella' term that encompasses a range of behaviours (Tokunaga, 2010). Currently, whilst there appears to be some agreement amongst academics and practitioners as to how to define face-to-face bullying, such agreement is lacking for cyberbullying. In particular, some authors argue that cyberbullying represents a distinct phenomenon which should be defined as such (e.g., Pieschl, Kuhlmann, & Prosch, 2015), whereas other authors advocate that cyberbullying is an extension of face-to-face bullying (e.g., Juvonen & Gross, 2008; Olweus, 2013) with researchers seeking to apply definitions of face-to-face bullying to cyberbullying (e.g., Calvete, Orue, Estévez, Villardón, & Padilla, 2010). However, this approach is limited because of the range of behaviours young people experience and engage in and the range of media they use. Moreover, digital technology is evolving and, as such, so too are the methods used to cyberbully others, a fact which must be acknowledged in definitions of cyberbullying. Therefore, Chap. 2 will discuss the range of media that can be used to cyberbully and the various behaviours and actions that constitute cyberbullying.

Chapter 3 will expand on some of the themes identified in Chap. 2 relating to how cyberbullying is defined. In particular, Chap. 3 will present a critical discussion of how cyberbullying differs from other forms of bullying and highlight the unique nature of cyberbullying. Specifically, attention will be paid to the power dynamics in the perpetrator (bully)–target (victim) relationship, the frequency of the acts, the role of anonymity, and the potentially relentless nature of cyberbullying. The chapter will also begin to explore some of the legalities of cyberbullying.

The reported prevalence rates of experiencing cyberbullying as a target vary from 1.5% (Ortega, Calmaetara, & Mora-Mechán, 2008) to 72% (Juvonen & Gross, 2008) and similar variations are seen for the reported prevalence of engaging in cyberbullying behaviours as a perpetrator. Chapter 4 will provide an overview of the reported prevalence rates of cyberbullying from contemporary academic literature. Whilst these variations may reflect actual differences in young people's experiences, Chap. 4 will also provide a critical exploration of the other factors that may account for this variation including: The methodology used to determine the prevalence rates, the time frame that is considered, and characteristics of the participants (including age, sex, and the country of study). The chapter will also present some of the reasons why young people may distort their reports of involvement in cyberbullying, including the fear of having their access to technology curtailed and social desirability. Alongside discussing the issues around the prevalence of cyberbullying, Chap. 4 will also review the factors that may predict young people's involvement in cyberbullying either as a target or perpetrator.

The short- and long-term consequences of involvement in face-to-face bullying have been well documented (e.g., Olweus, 2013; Smith, 2004), comparably fewer studies have examined the consequences of involvement in cyberbullying. To date, the majority of the research examining the consequences of involvement in cyberbullying has been cross-sectional in nature meaning that (1) the longer-term outcomes remain unclear, and (2) it is difficult to determine causality in these relationships. Notwithstanding these challenges, Chap. 5 will discuss the current literature that has explored the consequences of being involved in cyberbullying either as a target or a perpetrator. In particular, research has examined associations between cyberbullying involvement, psychosocial adjustment (including indicators of mental well-being, depression, anxiety, and social relationships), and general adjustment (including indicators of school performance and health). Generally speaking, the research has found that those who are involved in cyberbullying in some way experience both short- and long-term negative consequences. Chapter 5 will also consider the evidence that involvement in cyberbullying is predictive of suicide and further involvement in cyberbullying.

Chapter 6 will question what can be done to address cyberbullying. Numerous interventions have been developed that attempt to ameliorate the effects of face-to-face bullying. These interventions include whole school interventions, classroom-based interventions, and targeted interventions between the target and perpetrator. However, similar bespoke interventions designed to tackle cyberbullying have been reported to have limited success and impact. Chapter 6 will discuss some of the evidence-based interventions that have been developed to tackle cyberbullying. There is also ambiguity with regard to who should intervene in cyberbullying episodes, because cyberbullying often happens outside of school and the perpetrator of the behaviour is often anonymous. Therefore, establishing who is best placed to tackle cyberbullying warrants consideration and a range of guidance has been developed for key stakeholders involved in cyberbullying which will be reviewed in Chap. 6. Finally, Chap. 6 will also consider the legal position of cyberbullying.

Chapter 7 will draw together the main arguments and themes presented throughout this book. The chapter will present seven areas of development for future research examining cyberbullying, namely, the need (1) for a common definition of cyberbullying, (2) for agreement on the measures of cyberbullying, (3) to establish accurate prevalence rates of cyberbullying, (4) for longitudinal work to examine the consequences of cyberbullying, (5) to develop robust and empirically validated interventions, (6) to clarify the legal status of cyberbullying, and (7) to recognise that technology and cyberbullying is evolving.

References

Ang, R. P., Huan, V. S., & Florell, D. (2014). Understanding the relationship between proactive and reactive aggression, and cyberbullying across United States and Singapore adolescent samples. *Journal of Interpersonal Violence, 29*, 237–254.

Archer, J., & Coyne, S. M. (2005). An integrated review of indirect, relational, and social aggression. *Personality and Social Psychology Review, 9*, 212–230.

Bauman, S., & Bellmore, A. (2015). New directions in cyberbullying research. *Journal of School Violence, 14*, 1–10.

Beran, T. N., Rinaldi, C., Bickham, D. S., & Rich, M. (2012). Evidence for the need to support adolescents dealing with harassment and cyber-harassment: Prevalence, progression, and impact. *School Psychology International, 33*, 562–576.

Bowling, N. A., & Beehr, T. A. (2006). Workplace harassment from the victim's perspective: A theoretical model and meta-analysis. *Journal of Applied Psychology, 91*, 998–1012.

Bucchianeri, M. M., Eisenberg, M. E., & Neumark-Sztainer, D. (2013). Weightism, racism, classism, and sexism: Shared forms of harassment in adolescents. *Journal of Adolescent Health, 53*, 47–53.

Calvete, E., Orue, I., Estévez, A., Villardón, L., & Padilla, P. (2010). Cyberbullying in adolescents: Modalities and aggressors' profile. *Computers in Human Behavior, 26*, 1128–1135.

Card, N. A., & Little, T. D. (2006). Proactive and reactive aggression in childhood and adolescence: A meta-analysis of differential relations with psychosocial adjustment. *International Journal of Behavioral Development, 30*, 466–480.

Cassidy, W., Jackson, M., & Brown, K. N. (2009). Sticks and stones can break my bones, but how can pixels hurt me?: Students' experiences with cyber-bullying. *School Psychology International, 30,* 383–402.

Davies, K., Randall, D. P., Ambrose, A., & Orand, M. (2014). 'I was bullied too': Stories of bullying and coping in an online community. *Information, Communication & Society, 18,* 357–375.

Juvonen, J., & Gross, E. F. (2008). Extending the school grounds?—Bullying experiences in cyberspace. *Journal of School Health, 78,* 496–505.

Lee, E. (2009). The relationship of aggression and bullying to social preference: Differences in gender and types of aggression. *International Journal of Behavioral Development, 33,* 323–330.

Liu, J., Lewis, G., & Evans, L. (2013). Understanding aggressive behavior across the life span. *Journal of Psychiatric Mental Health Nursing, 20,* 156–168.

Moreno, G. (2011). Cases of victimization Case 3: Phoebe Prince (Massachusetts, 2010). *Preventing School Failure, 55,* 87.

Neall, A. M., & Tuckey, M. R. (2014). A methodological review of research on the antecedents and consequences of workplace harassment. *Journal of Occupational Psychology, 87,* 225–257.

Olweus, D. (2013). School bullying: Development and some important challenges. *Annual Review of Clinical Psychology, 9,* 751–780.

Ortega, R., Calmaestra, J., & Mora-Merchán, J. (2008). Cyberbullying. *International Journal of Psychology and Psychological Therapy, 8,* 183–192.

Orue, I., & Andershed, H. (2015). The Youth Psychopathic Traits Inventory-Short Version in Spanish adolescents—Factor structure, reliability, and relation with aggression, bullying, and cyber bullying. *Journal of Psychopathology and Behavioral Assessment, 37,* 563–575.

Pieschl, S., Kuhlmann, C., & Prosch, T. (2015). Beware of publicity! Perceived distress of negative cyber incidents and implications for defining cyberbullying. *Journal of School Violence, 14,* 111–132.

Raver, J. L., & Nishii, L. S. (2010). Once, twice, or three time as harmful? Ethnic harassment, gender harassment, and generalized workplace harassment. *Journal of Applied Psychology, 95,* 236–254.

Roland, E., & Idsøe, T. (2001). Aggression and bullying. *Aggressive Behavior, 27,* 446–462.

Smith, P. K. (2004). Bullying: Recent developments. *Child and Adolescent Mental Health, 9,* 98–103.

Tokunaga, R. S. (2010). Following you home from school: A critical review and synthesis of research on cyberbullying victimization. *Computers in Human Behavior, 26,* 277–287.

Zych, I., Ortega-Ruiz, R., & Del Rey, R. (2015). Scientific research on bullying and cyberbullying: Where we have been and where we are going. *Aggression and Violent Behavior, 24,* 188–198.

CHAPTER 2

Definitions of Cyberbullying

Abstract Across the academic literature, there is little agreement with regard to what constitutes cyberbullying, leading Tokunaga (*Computers in Human Behavior*, 26:277–287, 2010) to argue that the term is somewhat of an 'umbrella' phrase that encompasses online bullying, electronic bullying, and Internet harassment. Some definitions of cyberbullying have utilised definitions of face-to-face bullying as a foundation including elements of repetition, power imbalance, and intention. Other definitions highlight the distinct nature of cyberbullying behaviours and also acknowledge the various media through which it can occur. This chapter considers some of the debates surrounding the definition of cyberbullying and provides an overview of some of the contemporary definitions.

Keywords Cyberbullying • Definition • Conceptualisation • Media • Face-to-face bullying

This chapter will provide a concise overview of the current debates in the literature regarding how cyberbullying has been defined and operationalised by researchers, young people, educational practitioners, and key stakeholders. Cyberbullying has become somewhat of an 'umbrella' term that has been used to describe a range of behaviours, including online bullying, electronic bullying, and Internet harassment (Tokunaga, 2010).

© The Editor(s) (if applicable) and The Author(s) 2016   9
L.R. Betts, *Cyberbullying*, DOI 10.1057/978-1-137-50009-0_2

Therefore, having presented some of the contemporary definitions of cyberbullying and discussed the debate about the relationship between face-to-face bullying definitions and cyberbullying definitions, this chapter will also consider the media through which cyberbullying can occur, and the various behaviours and acts that may constitute cyberbullying. Finally, the chapter will end with a discussion of the emerging line of research that has begun to explore young people's understanding and the definitions of cyberbullying.

2.1   Defining Cyberbullying

Despite the pervasiveness of the term cyberbullying in our everyday vocabulary, there is little consensus within the academic literature as to which behaviours and experiences constitute cyberbullying. This lack of consistency and consensus has been attributed to the relative 'newness' of this form of bullying when compared to face-to-face bullying (Law, Shapka, Hymel, Oslon, & Waterhouse, 2012). Face-to-face bullying was first defined by Olweus in the 1970s (e.g., Olweus, 1978). Table 2.1 outlines some of the many different definitions of cyberbullying that researchers have presented.

The range of definitions of cyberbullying proposed by researchers reflects how technology has evolved over the last decade and how cyberbullying behaviours have, in turn, evolved with the technology. For example, the capabilities of mobile telephones have evolved rapidly from devices used to primarily send and receive small text message services and calls to devices that have 4G connectivity, as smart telephones capable of undertaking many of the functions of computers become the norm. Recent figures from the UK suggest that smart telephones are now the most popular media for going online (Ofcom, 2015). Reflecting these advances in the mobile communication industry, the mechanisms through which cyberbullying can occur via mobile telephones has evolved to include Internet-mediated communications. Additionally, other forms of portable devices, including tablets, have also become popular since 2003 when the term cyberbullying was first proposed.

To reflect this enhanced level of connectivity afforded by the latest smart telephones and other portable devices, and the evolving capabilities of many digital devices, some researchers, such as Tokunaga (2010), propose that a more holistic view of cyberbullying is required. Tokunaga argues that it is important to include aspects of aggression and hostile

Table 2.1 Some definitions of cyberbullying

Cyberbullying involves 'using ICTs to support intentional, recurrent and mean-spirited actions with the aim of harming others' (Akbulut et al., 2010, p. 47).

Cyberbullying behaviours are designed to 'embarrass, threaten, hurt, or exclude' (Bhat, 2008, p. 58).

Cyberbullying occurs when 'someone is tormented, threatened, harassed, humiliated, embarrassed or otherwise targeted' (Borgia & Myers, 2010, p. 29).

Cyberbullying involves 'repeated use of technology to harass, humiliate, or threaten' (Holladay, 2011, p. 4).

'Cyberbullying is defined as the intentional act of online/digital intimidation, embarrassment, or harassment' (Mark & Ratliffe, 2011, p. 92).

Cyberbullying is 'any peer-targeted aggressive behaviour via electronic communication technologies' (Mehari et al., 2014, p. 400).

Cyberbullying as 'willful and repeated harm inflicted through the medium of electronic text' (Patchin & Hinduja, 2006, p. 152).

Cyberbullying is 'repeated unwanted, hurtful, harassing, and/or threatening interaction through electronic communication media' (Rafferty & Vander Ven, 2014, p. 364).

Electronic bullying is 'a means of bullying in which peers use electronics to taunt, insult, threaten, harass, and/or intimidate a peer' (Raskauskas & Stoltz, 2007, p. 565).

'Cyberbullying is a systematic abuse of power which occurs through the use of information and communication technologies (ICTs)' (Slonje et al., 2013, p. 26).

'Cyberbullying is any behavior performed through electronic or digital media by individuals or groups that repeatedly communicates hostile or aggressive messages intended to inflict harm or discomfort on others' (Tokunaga, 2010, p. 278).

'Cyberbullying occurs when Internet-based applications are used to systematically intimidate or insult a person so as to humiliate, embarrass, or hurt that person. Similar to offline bullying, cyberbullying involves intentional repetitive actions and psychological violence' (Valkenburg & Peter, 2011, pp. 124–125).

Cyberbullying is 'a form of aggression that occurs through personal computers (e.g., e-mail and instant messaging) or cell phones (e.g., text messaging)' (Wang, Iannotti, & Nansel, 2009, p. 369).

"When we say cyberbullied, we mean bullied through email, instant messaging, social media, in a chat room, on a website, in an online game, or through a text message sent to a cell phone. For example someone who sends mean messages to another person in an email or posts negative comments or information about that person via social media, like Facebook, is cyberbullying" (Whittaker & Kowalski, 2015, p. 14).

and harmful acts as components of cyberbullying that can happen via an (unspecified) electronic device. Considering cyberbullying as something that occurs through any electronic device rather than a specified device has the advantage of potentially standing the test of time, because the evolving nature of technology is somewhat acknowledged in this approach. However, this flexibility is at the expense of gaining an understanding of (1) how young people experience cyberbullying through a specific device, and (2) whether different experiences occur according to the device. Consequently, it may be more appropriate to examine cyberbullying both in terms of general devices and also through separate devices. Greater consideration of the media through which cyberbullying can be experienced is discussed later in this chapter in Sect. 2.2.

Parallels have also been drawn between the definitions of face-to-face bullying and cyberbullying. It is widely accepted that bullying represents an intentional act that is repeated, and that there is an imbalance of power between the perpetrator of the act and the intended target of the act, who are peers or age-mates. Whilst researchers, such as Calvete, Orue, Estévez, Villardón, and Padilla (2010), argue that cyberbullying involves behaviours traditionally associated with face-to-face bullying such as insults, rumours, and threats that are communicated through an electronic medium; more recently, in a review of the bullying literature, Olweus (2013) took this proposition further.

Olweus (2013) argued that cyberbullying is the same as face-to-face bullying but that in the case of cyberbullying, the bullying episode occurs via electronic devices. Consequently, Olweus advocates that any definition of cyberbullying must be based on definitions of face-to-face bullying drawing on the principles of intention, repetition, and power imbalance between peers. Similarly, Smith (2009) has argued that cyberbullying is bullying by mobile telephone and the Internet. Therefore, definitions of cyberbullying have been proposed similar to those of Slonje, Smith, and Frisén (2013, see Table 2.1) that integrate these characteristics of intention, repetition, and power imbalance. However, as outlined in Chap. 3, there are some challenges associated with simply translating definitions of face-to-face bullying to the digital environment because of some of the unique aspects of cyberbullying.

Face-to-face bullying is regarded as an abusive relationship that involves repeated, intentionally hurtful acts directed towards a target who is less powerful than the perpetrator and, as such, is unable to defend themselves (Smith, 2009). Although equivalences have been highlighted between the definitions of face-to-face bullying and cyberbullying at the global level with regard to intention, repetition, and power imbalance, some researchers argue that cyberbullying aligns more closely to specific forms of face-to-face bullying. Face-to-face bullying can take many forms such as verbal, relational, social, and physical which depend on the behaviour that an individual experiences, and engages in, during the bullying episode (Hawker & Boulton, 2000). Examples of verbal bullying include making rude comments, name-calling, teasing, taunting, and mocking the target. Relational bullying involves trying to disrupt the social relationships of the target either through spreading rumours, excluding the target, or some other action that undermines the target's status within the social arena. Social bullying is distinguished from other forms of face-to-face bullying because it also involves non-verbal cues to indicate intent in addition to rumour spreading, backbiting, and social exclusion (Coyne, Archer, & Eslea, 2006). Physical bullying occurs when an individual is attacked in some way such as being hit, punched, or kicked. Mynard and Joseph (2000) also proposed that face-to-face peer bullying can include attacks on property where the personal possessions of the target are damaged by the perpetrator. Mark and Ratliffe (2011) argue that cyberbullying reflects a relatively new form of relational bullying because it uses technology to carry out many acts traditionally associated with relational bullying. For example, name-calling, threats, spreading rumours, disclosing the target's personal/confidential information without their permission, social isolation, and exclusion are all acts of relational bullying that can be carried out via technology. Similarly, Wang, Iannotti, and Luk (2012) also argued that cyberbullying may be similar to face-to-face relational bullying because both involve verbal bullying, social exclusion, and spreading rumours.

The distinction has also been made between face-to-face bullying behaviours that are direct versus indirect. Direct bullying occurs as part of a face-to-face interaction, whereas indirect bullying occurs via a third party (Rivers & Smith, 1994). Therefore, the recipient of direct face-to-face bullying is the target of the bullying episode such that the behaviour of the perpetrator occurs in the presence of the target and the target is aware of what is happening. With indirect face-to-face bullying, the bullying episode may happen without the targets' knowledge and does not occur in the presence of the target. Consequently, indirect face-to-face bullying can be considered to occur behind the targets' back. Similar to face-to-face bullying, cyberbullying can also be direct or indirect (Vandebosch & van Cleemput, 2009). Direct cyberbullying includes physical (e.g., purposely sending a virus-infected file), verbal (e.g., using the Internet or mobile telephone to insult or threaten), non-verbal (e.g., sending threatening or obscene pictures of illustrations), and social (e.g., excluding someone from a group online). Indirect cyberbullying includes 'outing' of entrusted information; masquerading (e.g., deceiving someone by pretending to be someone else); spreading gossip by mobile telephone, email, or chat; and taking part in voting on a defamatory polling websites. Cyberbullying has also been regarded as a covert form of verbal and written bullying (Mason, 2008). Parallels have also been drawn between covert face-to-face bullying and cyberbullying. For example, cyberbullying can be regarded as a form of covert bullying especially when the perpetrator is anonymous or the target is unable to respond (Spears, Slee, Owens, & Johnson, 2009). Further, Spears et al. make the comparison between bashboards and anonymous voting booths that allow anonymous written comments to be left by the perpetrator about a target as similar to notes that would have previously been passed round school.

In addition to the discussed similarities between face-to-face bullying and cyberbullying, another reason why cyberbullying has been considered by some researchers to be an extension of face-to-face bullying that uses technology as a mechanism to target others is that there is some evidence that the targets have the same perpetrators in both the 'real' and the 'virtual' world (Wegge, Vandebosch, & Eggermont, 2014). However, as discussed in Chaps. 3 and 4, the prevalence rates of cyberbullying and unique characteristics of cyberbullying mean that this may be an oversimplification of the similarities between the two forms of bullying.

In contrast to those researchers who argue that cyberbullying is an extension of face-to-face bullying that uses technology (e.g., Olweus, 2013), other researchers argue that cyberbullying represents a distinct and separate phenomenon that should not be confounded with face-to-face bullying (Pieschl, Kuhlmann, & Prosch, 2015). For example, there is evidence that American students regard cyberbullying as a distinct experience from overt and relational forms of face-to-face bullying (Dempsey, Sulkowski, Nichols, & Storch, 2009). Similarly, Dooley, Pyzalski, and Cross (2009) argue that it is important to conceptualise cyberbullying as distinct from face-to-face bullying to ensure that the intricacies of the behaviours that constitute cyberbullying are fully explored. These intricacies are likely to include the power imbalance, repetition, and the nature of the act and technology used. Further, Huang and Chou (2010) advocate that the evolving digital world and the pervasiveness of technology means that bullying is occurring in a new space and, as such, has transformed into a new form. Therefore, it has been argued that cyberbullying does not simply constitute an electronic form of aggression or an extension of face-to-face bullying but is rather a separate phenomenon. In support of this proposition, Pieschl et al. recently argued that many of the defining characteristics of face-to-face bullying may not apply to cyberbullying, may behave differently in cyberbullying, or may require additional clarification. Consequently, according to these researchers, it is not appropriate to simply take a definition of face-to-face bullying and apply it to the digital world, but rather it is important to explore the potential harm and socio-emotional distress caused by experiencing cyberbullying.

A recent meta-analysis of cyberbullying research undertaken by Kowalski, Giumetti, Schroeder, and Lattanner (2014) argued that the definitions of cyberbullying comprised four distinct components: '(a) intentional aggressive behaviour that is (b) carried out repeatedly, (c) occurs between a perpetrator and victim who are unequal in power, and (d) occurs through electronic technologies' (p. 37). Whilst these four components resonate with the definitions of face-to-face bullying previously discussed, research often fails to address all of these components when defining and assessing cyberbullying. In particular, repetition and power imbalance are often not fully operationalised in the measures designed to assess cyberbullying. Although one way of assessing whether an act is repeated could be to ask respondents to self-report the frequency of the incident, as discussed in Chap. 3 Sect. 3.2, repetition has a distinct meaning in the context of cyberbullying. Notwithstanding the challenges of how repetition is operationalised in cyberbullying, assessing whether an aggressive act is repeated enables researchers to make the distinction between cyber harassment and cyberbullying (Machackova, Cerna, Sevcikova, Dedkova, & Daneback, 2013). Using this distinction, cyber harassment is seen as a one-off act of aggression, whereas cyberbullying is seen as repeated acts of aggression.

More recently, Thomas, Connor, and Scott (2015) argued that whilst cyberbullying is characterised by a power imbalance and repetition, the anonymity and the potentially public nature of cyberbullying should be considered as more important facets in the definitions of cyberbullying than they currently are. In comparison to face-to-face bullying which typically is undertaken by a perpetrator known to the target with a limited audience, and constrained by geography, with cyberbullying, the true identity of the perpetrator may be unknown to the target and the acts could potentially be witnessed by an unlimited and worldwide audience. The unlimited audience for cyberbullying may also not be constrained by time and space, such that they could witness cyberbullying after the episode had initially occurred. Further, the anonymity and public nature of acts associated with cyberbullying may indirectly contribute to the power imbalance in cyberbullying. It may be that adopting such an operationalisation of the power imbalance of cyberbullying is appropriate because, unlike face-to-face bullying which may rely on physical power differences, power in cyberbullying may be associated with knowledge differences or the fear created in the target (for a further discussion on this area, please see Chap. 3 Sect. 3.4).

The importance of the repetition of acts directed towards a target to characterise cyberbullying versus a one-off act of electronic aggression was further elucidated by Pyzalski (2012). Pyzalski, in consultation with 15-year-olds from Poland, proposed a typology of electronic aggression. The typology included six different types of electronic aggression that varied according to the target, perpetrator, and the targets' knowledge of the acts:

1. *Electronic peer aggression* occurred between young people as both the target and perpetrator, and, if repeated, could escalate into cyberbullying;
2. *Electronic aggression against school staff* targeted staff at the school where the perpetrator attended;
3. *Electronic aggression against the vulnerable* targeted 'weaker' individuals who were not aware of the aggression directed towards them. Pyzalski argued that this type of aggression was often directed towards the homeless or those with substance dependence and could involve visual images of the target(s);
4. *Random electronic aggression* occurred when the target of the aggression was anonymous to the perpetrator and the targets were often selected on impulse. Specifically, these targets were likely to be fellow forum or chatroom users who happened to find themselves in the same virtual space as the perpetrator;
5. *Electronic aggression against groups* involved particular social groups being targeted, and the behaviour was likely to cause offence amongst group members. Targets of this form of aggression could include groups based on ethnicity or their religious beliefs and, whilst this behaviour is not directed at a specific individual within the group, the entire group may feel offended; and
6. *Electronic aggression against celebrities* involved targeting well-known individuals, and when this occurred through the use of 'gossip' portals, it was considered to be indirect aggression.

Patchin and Hinduja (2015) argue that the lack of clarity concerning how cyberbullying has been defined has resulted in a misunderstanding of the phenomenon and undermines our ability to identify, prevent, and tackle cyberbullying. Whilst there seem to be common themes that have emerged from the definitions of cyberbullying with regard to harmful acts, repetition, power imbalance, and the use of digital technology, it is important to acknowledge that multiple forms of technology exist. Given the array of technology and the many platforms that young people use, it may be that young people's experiences of cyberbullying vary according to the media through which they experience cyberbullying. The next section of this chapter will turn its attention to the nature of the media and how this potentially impacts on the definitions of cyberbullying.

2.2 MEDIA

The mechanisms and media through which cyberbullying can be experienced has also evolved with technology since 2003. This evolution of cyberbullying is likely to continue as new forms of technology and new trends of use continue to emerge (Slonje et al., 2013). For example, Beale and Hall (2007) suggested that instant messengers, social networking sites, email, small text messaging, websites, voting booths, chatrooms, and bashrooms (a bulletin board where users can post anonymous comments) could all be used as mediums to cyberbully others. Given that this list of media was proposed in 2007, it is important to recognise that with the advances of digital technology, there have also been changes in the perceived popularity of different forms of media and different platforms during this time. For example, Robards (2012) documents that transition made by Australian youth away from MySpace to Facebook, as Facebook became the site of choice during the late 2000s. Robards argues that this transition occurred because of the functionality of the sites, and social pressures meant that Facebook became the site of choice. Conversely, Boyd (2011) argues that young people's choice of social network sites, and the relative popularity of Facebook versus MySpace in American youth, reflects a deeper societal division according to race and social inequality.

Notwithstanding the changing preferences, in terms of which particular version of the media is *en vogue* with young people, it is likely that similar mechanisms can be used to cyberbully others. Bhat (2008) proposed a number of mechanisms through which cyberbullying can occur for a range of media. For example, fake accounts can be created using instant messenger systems to exclude individuals from their peer network or to spread messages. Mobile telephones can be used to forward personal text messages, picture messages, and videos about the target without their permission or consent for the content. Chatrooms can be used to embarrass, threaten, shame, or engage a target in sexual conversations. Emails containing verbal, audio, and visual material can be used to disseminate information to a large audience. Similarly, social networking sites and blogs can reach a large audience and can be used to embarrass, humiliate, or attack an individual. In a recent study with female 12- to 15-year-olds, Kernaghan and Elwood (2013) reported that the participants experienced cyberbullying through instant messenger and social networking sites. Together, these media were used to impersonate others, send hurtful or malicious messages, and share private or embarrassing information. It is important to acknowledge that the devices through which these actions could be facilitated include computers, tablets, and smart telephones.

As outlined above a range of media can be used by young people to engage in cyberbullying. Therefore, researchers such as Calvete et al. (2010) advocate that, rather than exploring cyberbullying in general terms across all media simultaneously, cyberbullying should be examined for individual media and that a broad array of media should be included in such assessments. In practical terms this would involve asking young people to report the media that they use and then, for each media, report their experiences of cyberbullying. However, Slonje et al. (2013) caution researchers to be careful of how they operationalise the definition of cyberbullying to different media. For example, whilst the distinction between cyberbullying via mobile telephones and cyberbullying via the Internet may have been appropriate previously, because of the changing capabilities of portable devices, this distinction is less appropriate than it once was. Another reason why researchers need to be cautious when examining cyberbullying across a range of media is that the popularity of different media is consistently changing as new platforms and devices become available and as fashions shift. Consequently, it is also possible that new forms of cyberbullying will evolve as technology continues to evolve. Together, these caveats with regard to specific media have prompted some researchers to argue that it is more appropriate to explore cyberbullying in terms of the behaviours and individual experiences rather than the media through which these behaviours and experiences occur (e.g., Rivers, 2013). The next section of the chapter will consider the various behaviours that researchers and practitioners have advocated to be indicative of cyberbullying.

2.3 BEHAVIOURS

Exploring the behaviours that individuals engage in and experience in the digital world also offers a different insight into cyberbullying. Slonje et al. (2013) argue that it is important that researchers examine the nature and content of a cyberbullying act as well as the medium through which it occurs. Similarly, Mehari, Farrel, and Le (2014) also recommend that when examining cyberbullying, it is necessary to explore both a range of behaviours and media to reflect the types of technology that young people use.

Willard (2007) proposed eight types of behaviour that she argued differentiated between cyberbullying behaviours: flaming, harassment, denigration, impersonation, outing and trickery, exclusion, cyberstalking, and cyberthreats. Flaming typically occurs in public environments and is a heated argument or threatening and insulting interaction that can occur between individuals or small groups. Unlike flaming, harassment involves repeated messages to a specific individual who is the target over a sustained period of time. Denigration occurs when harmful or untrue comments or gossip are circulated about an individual with the ultimate goal of disrupting or damaging their social network. The targets of denigration are often unaware of the behaviour that is directed towards them. Whilst Willard initially argued that denigration occurs through text based communication, images are increasingly being used to denigrate others. Impersonation involves an individual or group pretending to be the target with the explicit aim of portraying the target in a negative light to others. Outing and trickery are linked behaviours. Outing involves the distribution of personal communications, disclosures, or images beyond the original scope. Trickery occurs when an individual discloses information or images believing that they are only for the recipient. However, the intended recipient subsequently distributes the information, communication, or images to others. Exclusion occurs when individuals purposefully leave the target out of, or block them from, activities.

Cyberstalking can involve many of the previously mentioned acts outlined by Willard (2007) and occurs when an individual experiences denigration, exclusion, or is repeatedly targeted either through threatening, intimidating, or offensive messages. In particular, cyberstalking often involves repeated attacks on the individual that moves beyond harassment because the target begins to fear for their safety. Willard also makes the distinction between two forms of cyberthreats: direct threats and distressing material. Direct threats relate to communication of intent to hurt someone, whereas distressing material pertains to emotionally rich communication that indicates someone is considering hurting someone or themselves. Some of the behaviours outlined by Willard, whilst not labelled cyberbullying, can be considered to be cyberbullying. For example, cyber harassment could develop into cyberbullying. Other acts that have been regarded as cyberbullying include programming-infected software, hacking, or spreading infected emails (Aricak et al., 2008). Similarly, cyberbullying has been regarded as harassment, abuse, insult, teasing, and blackmail via digital technology (Katzer, Fetchenhauer, & Belschak, 2009).

More recently, Chisholm (2014) proposed 11 different behavioural acts that constitute cyberbullying:

1. Catfishing—tricking people into relationships by creating false identities and social networks;
2. Cheating, forming roving gangs, and blocking entry points in massive multiplayer online games;
3. Spreading insults and humiliating or threatening messages or images to an online community;
4. Flaming—purposively adopting an argumentative interactional style;
5. Impersonating others;
6. Slamming—bystanders engaging in harassment that they did not initiate;
7. Ratting—controlling a target's device without their knowledge to access files, spy, or control the device;
8. Relational aggression—spreading rumours, excluding the target, deleting the target from a friendship list, or posting threats;
9. Sexting—distributing sexually suggestive images;
10. Shock trolling—creating offensive posts online with the intention of provoking a anger, frustration, or humiliation response; and
11. Stalking online or threatening violence.

In line with Chisholm's (2014) conceptualisation of the behaviours that are indicative of cyberbullying, sexting or the distributing of sexually suggestive images beyond the originally intended recipient has played a role in high profile cases of cyberbullying, for example, the case of Jesse Logan (Moreno, 2011). Jesse sent her boyfriend nude images of herself and then when the relationship broke down, her ex-boyfriend then made the images available to other school mates who then, in turn, ridiculed Jesse. Following Jesse's experience, she then committed suicide which was partly attributed to the cyberbullying that she had experienced through the distribution of the images beyond their original audience. Jesse's experiences also has parallels with a recent trend termed 'revenge porn' where on the breakdown of relationships, previous partners are distributing sexually suggestive and explicit images of their ex-partner (Stokes, 2014).

Despite the wealth of behaviours that have been discussed so far in this chapter, when researchers have investigated the behaviours that young people engage in with regard to cyberbullying, a slightly different picture emerges. A recent study undertaken by Garaigordobil (2015), with young people from Spain, found that the most frequently reported behaviours associated with cyberbullying were stealing someone's password, anonymous frightening telephone calls, sending offensive or insulting messages, and slandering by lying about someone in order to discredit them.

Whilst a number of behaviours may constitute cyberbullying, Akbulut, Sahin, and Eristi (2010) argue that the context in which behaviours are experienced underpins how a young person interprets whether the behaviour constitutes an act of cyberbullying. For example, when behaviours or acts are perceived as less personally targeted towards the individual but rather targeted to a larger and potentially ambiguous audience (e.g., obscene images in webpages or popups, spam, and propaganda) or when friendship requests are made from unknown individuals through social media, these acts are deemed by young people not to be cyberbullying. However, when similar messages are directed to an individual via instant messenger or email or when messages are received from an unknown sender that included sexual allusion, they are interpreted as cyberbullying. Similarly, Facebook Rape or 'Frape' which involves making alterations to a target's Facebook account when the target has left their device logged on without their permission or knowledge is not regarded as cyberbullying (Pedersen, 2013).

In addition to making a distinction between the various forms of behaviours with regard to what constitutes cyberbullying, there is also evidence that young people differentiate between the perceived seriousness of cyberbullying acts. For example, Vandebosch and van Cleemput (2009) reported that primary- and secondary- school-aged pupils identified the most hurtful forms of cyberbullying: to be breaking into the targets' computer and stealing personal information; disseminating private or protected information about the target via the Internet or mobile telephone;

online posting or forwarding by email and text confidential information; and spreading gossip by email or telephone. Therefore, because different acts of cyberbullying are perceived to vary with regard to the severity of the acts according to the individual, researchers should consider assessing the perceived severity of the cyberbullying acts to capture these individual differences.

Although a range of behaviours have been examined by researchers and educational practitioners, and various forms of behaviours have been conceptualised as being indicative of cyberbullying, it is important to consider how young people perceive cyberbullying. One reason for this is that as technology use continues to evolve, researchers and educational practitioners may not be fully aware of how young people are engaging with technology. Consequently, the next section of this chapter will explore young people's perceptions of cyberbullying.

2.4   Young People's Understanding of Cyberbullying

Researchers have recently begun to explore definitions of cyberbullying from the perspective of young people. There are at least two explanations for this line of research. First, exploring young people's understanding and conceptualisation of cyberbullying will ensure that measures designed to assess cyberbullying accurately reflect what behaviours young people experience and engage in. Adopting such an approach adheres to scale development guidelines to ensure that robust and psychometrically sound measures are developed to assess cyberbullying. Second, exploring young people's conceptualisation of cyberbullying is appropriate because many young people, researchers, and educational practitioners regard cyberbullying to be more problematic than face-to-face bullying (Mishna, Saini, & Solomon, 2009).

Whilst young people regard cyberbullying as problematic, they also recognise that some of the behaviours which have been considered to be cyberbullying can also be a routine part of many social interactions and that what distinguishes these behaviours is the underlying motives (Bryce & Fraser, 2013). Young people aged 11–15 years old also easily make, and articulate, the distinction between cyberbullying and 'banter' (Spenser & Betts, 2014). These young people regard cyberbullying as an extension of face-to-face bullying that uses digital means to: (1) share personal or private information, (2) blame an individual for something that they could not help, and (3) target an individual for something that they had said. Conversely, banter between friends was regarded as fun. This is consistent with how banter is regarded as a form of playful interactions between known individuals (Dynel, 2008). Similarly, Spanish adolescents regarded verbal and visual aggression as mechanisms that foster communication and facilitate interactions rather than cyberbullying behaviours (Cuadrado-Gordilllo & Fernández-Antelo, 2016). For this group of young people, cyberbullying was regarded as behaviours with an intent to cause harm, an imbalance of power, and advertising.

In other research that has sought to understand how young people conceptualise and define cyberbullying, Nocentini et al. (2010) undertook focus groups with young people, aged between 11 and 18, recruited from Italy, Spain, and Germany. The authors argued that for young people to determine whether a behaviour was cyberbullying, it was important to consider whether the act was intended to cause harm to the target, the effect of the act on the target, and the repetition of the act. Based on the young people's accounts, a typology of four main types of cyberbullying was created: written-verbal behaviours (including telephone calls, text messages, instant messengers, chatrooms, blogs, and social networking sites); visual behaviours (including posting, sending, or sharing compromising pictures and videos through mobile telephones or the Internet); exclusion (including purposefully excluding someone from an online group); and impersonation (including stealing and revealing personal information using another person's name and account).

It is also important to recognise that different young people may interpret the same behaviour in different ways. Specifically, a behaviour may be perceived in the way that it was intended by the perpetrator or the behaviour may be interpreted differently by the target than how the perpetrator had originally intended. For example, what perpetrators had intended to be cyberbullying may instead be interpreted by their targets not as cyberbullying but rather as teasing (Dehue, Bolman, & Völlink, 2008). Conversely, acts with a benign intent may be misconstrued to be an act of cyberbullying. Further, interpretation of intent may also extend beyond that the target and perpetrator such that the social norms of the group may also dictate whether an act is interpreted as cyberbullying. The social norms of the group may be group defined or may be more closely governed by external forces such as social desirability.

One explanation for this individual difference in how young people perceive hostility and intent is the attribution of intent they make to a specific act. The social information processing model (Crick & Dodge, 1994) states that children move through a six-stage process when they interact with others in the social world. The first stage involves the children encoding external and internal cues about the behaviour that they had just experienced. Following the encoding process, children then develop and interpret a mental representation of the cues such that they selectively attend to the aspects that they perceive to be relevant. This process is guided by memory but may involve a personalised mental representation, a causal analysis of the events, inferences about the perspectives of others, evaluations of efficacy, and inferences about the meaning of the peer. The next part of the process involves the child clarifying the goal of the behaviour or selecting the most appropriate goal for the situation. Next, if the situation has been encountered previously, then the child will select an appropriate response from their memory, or if the situation is new, then they will construct a new response to deal with the situation. The child then decides which is the most appropriate response, and this decision is guided by their degree of confidence and ability to enact the appropriate response. The final stage of the process involves children enacting the behaviour.

Whilst the social information processing model has been used to explain a response to a range of behaviours, it is important to recognise that the behaviour that a young person ultimately selects can be influenced by their own biases. An example of a bias that may arise in this situation is a hostile attribution bias (Orobio de Castro, Veerman, Koops, Bouch, & Monshouwer, 2002). The hostile attribution bias is the tendency, in ambiguous situations, for aggressive individuals to attribute aggression as the motivation for a particular behaviour and, as such, respond in an aggressive manner. Therefore, when these individuals with a predisposition to aggressive/hostile acts experience an ambiguous event, they are more likely to misattribute the cause and respond inappropriately with aggression. The hostile attribution bias has been used to explain responses to face-to-face bullying (Dodge, 2006), and the approach can also be applied to some forms of technology mediated communication. Specifically, the hostile attribution bias is particularly relevant to media such as text messages where content can be misinterpreted because of the limited information (Allen, 2012). Allen reports that females are more likely to interpret text messages as hostile, and this is likely to lead to conflict and 'drama' which may then contribute to cyberbullying. Specifically, 'drama' is a form of social interaction that is characterised by an overreaction and excessive emotionality where the relevance of a situation is overinflated and the situation receives more attention and importance than is warranted (Allen, 2012). The link between drama and cyberbullying is proposed because drama typically involves gossip and rumours which is similar to the behaviours associated with cyberbullying.

Adopting qualitative methods with young people, Vandebosch and Van Cleemput (2008) reported that young people consider cyberbullying to be an intentional act that is designed to cause hurt, that is repeated, and there is a power imbalance between the target and the perpetrator. Spears et al. (2009) undertook a similar qualitative study and the results revealed that the young people understood the power differential in cyberbullying. The power differential was associated with the sense of helplessness felt when an individual experiences cyberbullying. The findings also suggested that covert cyberbullying could be indirect, social, or relational actions that lead to exclusion, isolation, and manipulation of social networks. Typically, such actions would involve rumours, image sharing when the target does not know, anonymous derogatory websites, or cyberbullying from an anonymous perpetrator. Overt cyberbullying was suggested to be deliberately taking intimate images and sharing images to cause harm to the target or using technology to cause harm. Finally, Spears et al. reported that different patterns of cyberbullying were discussed according to the age of the participants. Younger participants discussed cyberbullying with regard to friendship and social network manipulation, and attacks on social status, whereas older students were more to do with sexuality and sexual experiences such as sharing of images or sexual situations were filmed without the targets' knowledge.

Although there are many reasons why it may be preferable for researchers to use definitions and conceptualisations of cyberbullying that young people have been involved in generating, there are challenges associated with adopting such an approach. For example, as Pieschl et al. (2015) note, one of the challenges associated with adopting a participant-driven definition of cyberbullying is that recent generations of young people have been actively taught about what constitutes bullying and how bullying can be defined. For example, it has been a legal requirement for all schools within the UK to have an anti-bullying policy. A content analysis of the documents reveals that cyberbullying was only mentioned in 32% of these in 2008 (Smith et al., 2012), with 52% of secondary schools mentioning cyberbullying in their anti-bullying policies. However, whilst some readers may regard these figures as low, they compare to less than 9% of anti-bullying policies mentioning cyberbullying in 2002 (Smith et al., 2012).

Despite what the academic literature tells us about which behaviours constitute cyberbullying, young people undoubtedly have an understanding of which behaviours comprise cyberbullying. Whether this awareness is from lessons learnt in educational establishments or from the media it may be that, as Pieschl et al. (2015) argue, young people are relying on their existing knowledge and these taught definitions when they are asked to discuss and conceptualise cyberbullying. Consequently, researchers need to be mindful of the information young people have received about cyberbullying when asking them to define cyberbullying. One practical way that researchers could address this issue is by asking young people to extend their definitions beyond what they have typically learnt at school and asking them to identify the source of the information that they have used when putting the definitions together.

In conclusion, this chapter has summarised some of the current debates about the appropriateness of definitions of cyberbullying that currently exist within the academic literature. Cyberbullying represents somewhat of a new phenomenon that first appeared in the academic literature in 2003, and despite numerous studies in this area that have sought to gain an understanding regarding how to appropriately define cyberbullying, there is little consensus in the literature. In particular, there is debate regarding both how to define and operationalise the term. Some researchers such as Olweus (2013) have argued that cyberbullying is an extension of face-to-face bullying and, as such, should include aspects of repetition, power imbalance, and intention in the definition. Conversely, other researchers have argued that cyberbullying is a distinct phenomenon which must be conceptualised as such in order to fully address the topic (Dooley et al., 2009; Pieschl et al., 2015).

In addition to whether cyberbullying definitions should make reference to intent, repetition, and imbalance of power, debate has also taken place as to whether cyberbullying should be regarded as the same across all media or whether it is more appropriate to examine cyberbullying according to specific media. The premise for exploring cyberbullying according to media and behaviours experienced is to enable researchers to gain a clearer understanding of what young people actually experience such that a young person-centric rather than a researcher-centric approach to cyberbullying is adopted. However, regardless of which conceptualisation of cyberbullying researchers and practitioners adopt, it is imperative that they consider how the population they are working with define and experience cyberbullying. Adopting such a participant driven approach will ensure that researchers explore what young people experience rather than what researchers think they experience. Further, a participant driven definition and conceptualisation of cyberbullying will also go some way to address the challenges associated with evolving technologies, preferences, and norms concerning technology use. However, it is important to note that adopting such a participant-centred approach may add additional complexities whilst trying to compare prevalence rates (see Chap. 4) and that the definitions of cyberbullying may also rely heavily on what young people have been taught at school.

REFERENCES

Akbulut, Y., Sahin, Y. L., & Eristi, B. (2010). Development of a scale to investigate cybervictimization among online social utility members. *Contemporary Educational Technology, 1*, 46–59.

Allen, K. P. (2012). Off the radar and ubiquitous: Text messaging and its relationship to 'drama' and cyberbullying in an affluent, academically rigorous US high school. *Journal of Youth Studies, 15*, 99–117.

Aricak, T., Siyahhan, S., Uzunhasanoglu, A., Saribeyoglu, S., Ciplak, S., Yilmaz, N., & Memmedov, C. (2008). Cyberbullying among Turkish adolescents. *CyberPsychology & Behavior, 11*, 253–261.

Beale, A. V., & Hall, K. R. (2007). Cyberbullying: What school administrators (and parents) can do. *Clearing House, 18*, 8–12.

Bhat, C. S. (2008). Cyber bullying: Overview and strategies for school counsellors, guidance officers, and all school personnel. *Australian Journal of Guidance & Counselling, 18*, 53–66.

Borgia, L. G., & Myers, J. J. (2010). Cyber safety and children's literature: A good match for creating classroom communities. *Illinois Reading Council Journal, 38*, 29–34.

Boyd, D. (2011). White flight in networked publics? How race and class shaped American teen engagement with MySpace and Facebook. In L. Nakamura & P. A. Chow-White (Eds.), *Race after the internet* (pp. 203–222). New York: Routledge.

Bryce, J., & Fraser, J. (2013). "It's common sense that it's wrong": Young people's perceptions and experiences of cyberbullying. *Cyberpsychology, Behavior, and Social Networking, 16*, 783–787.

Calvete, E., Orue, I., Estévez, A., Villardón, L., & Padilla, P. (2010). Cyberbullying in adolescents: Modalities and aggressors' profile. *Computers in Human Behavior, 26*, 1128–1135.

Chisholm, J. F. (2014). Review of the status of cyberbullying and cyberbullying prevention. *Journal of Information Systems Education, 25,* 77–87.

Coyne, S. M., Archer, J., & Eslea, M. (2006). "We're not friends anymore! Unless..." The frequency and harmfulness of indirect, relational. *Aggressive Behaviour, 32,* 294–307.

Crick, N. R., & Dodge, K. A. (1994). A review and reformulation of social information-processing mechanisms in children's social adjustment. *Psychological Bulletin, 115,* 74–101.

Cuadrado-Gordillo, I., & Fernández-Antelo, I. (2016). Adolescents' perception of the characterizing dimensions of cyberbullying: Differentiation between bullies' and victims' perceptions. *Computers in Human Behavior, 55,* 653–663.

Dehue, F., Bolman, C., & Völlink, T. (2008). Cyberbullying: Youngsters' experiences and parental perception. *CyberPsychology & Behavior, 11,* 217–223.

Dempsey, A. G., Sulkowski, M. L., Nichols, R., & Storch, E. A. (2009). Differences between peer victimization in cyber and physical settings and associated psychosocial adjustment in early adolescence. *Psychology in the Schools, 46,* 962–972.

Dodge, K. A. (2006). Translational science in action: Hostile attributional style and the development of aggressive behavior problems. *Developmental Psychopathology, 18,* 791–814.

Dooley, J. J., Pyżalski, J., & Cross, D. (2009). Cyberbullying versus face-to-face bullying: A theoretical and conceptual review. *Zeitschrift für Psychologie/Journal of Psychology, 217,* 182–188.

Dynel, M. (2008). No aggression, only teasing: The pragmatics of teasing and banter. *Lodz Papers in Pragmatics, 4,* 241–261.

Garaigordobil, M. (2015). Cyberbullying in adolescents and youth in the Basque country: Prevalence of cybervictims, cyberaggressors, and cyberobservers. *Journal of Youth Studies, 18,* 569–582.

Hawker, D. S. J., & Boulton, M. J. (2000). Twenty years' research on peer victimization and psychosocial maladjustment: A meta-analytic review of cross-sectional studies. *Journal of Child Psychology and Psychiatry, and Allied Disciplines, 41,* 441–455.

Holladay, J. (2011). Cyberbullying the stakes have never been higher for students or schools. *Teaching Tolerance, 38,* 42–45.

Huang, Y.-Y., & Chou, C. (2010). An analysis of multiple factors of cyberbullying among junior high school students in Taiwan. *Computers in Human Behavior, 26,* 1581–1590.

Katzer, C., Fetchenhauer, D., & Belschak, F. (2009). Cyberbullying: Who are the victims? A comparison of victimization in internet chatrooms and victimization in school. *Journal of Media Psychology, 21,* 25–36.

Kernaghan, D., & Elwood, J. (2013). All the (cyber) world's a stage: Framing cyberbullying as a performance. *Cyberpsychology: Journal of Psychosocial Research on Cyberspace, 7,* 1, article 5.

Kowalski, R. M., Giumetti, G. W., Schroeder, A. N., & Lattanner, M. R. (2014). Bulling in the digital age: A critical review and meta-analysis of cyberbullying research among youth. *Psychological Bulletin, 140*, 1073–1137.

Law, D. M., Shapka, J. D., Hymel, S., Olson, B. F., & Waterhouse, T. (2012). The changing face of bullying: An empirical comparison between traditional and internet bullying and victimization. *Computers in Human Behavior, 28*, 226–232.

Machackova, H., Cerna, A., Sevcikova, A., Dedkova, L., & Daneback, K. (2013). Effectiveness of coping strategies for victims of cyberbullying. *Cyberpsychology: Journal of Psychosocial Research on Cyberspace, 7*, 3, article 5.

Mark, L., & Ratliffe, K. T. (2011). Cyber worlds: New playgrounds for bullying. *Computers in the Schools, 28*, 92–116.

Mason, K. L. (2008). Cyberbullying: A preliminary assessment for school personnel. *Psychology in the Schools, 45*, 323–348.

Mehari, K. R., Farrell, A. D., & Le, A.-T. H. (2014). Cyberbullying among adolescents: Measures in search of a construct. *Psychology of Violence, 4*, 399–415.

Mishna, F., Saini, M., & Solomon, S. (2009). Ongoing and online: Children and youth's perceptions of cyber bullying. *Children and Youth Services Review, 31*, 1222–1228.

Moreno, G. (2011). Cases of victimization Case 4: Jesse Logan (Ohio, 2008). *Preventing School Failure, 55*, 87.

Mynard, H., & Joseph, S. (2000). Development of the multidimensional peer-victimization scale. *Aggressive Behavior, 26*, 169–178.

Nocentini, A., Calmaestra, J., Schultze-Krumbholz, A., Scheithauer, H., Ortega, R., & Menesini, E. (2010). Cyberbullying: Labels, behaviours and definition in three European countries. *Australian Journal of Guidance & Counselling, 20*, 129–142.

Ofcom. (2015). *The communications market report.* Retrieved August 11, 2015, from http://stakeholders.ofcom.org.uk/binaries/research/cmr/cmr15/CMR_UK_2015.pdf

Olweus, D. (1978). *Aggression in the schools: Bullies and whipping boys.* Washington, DC: Hemisphere (Wiley).

Olweus, D. (2013). School bullying: Development and some important challenges. *Annual Review of Clinical Psychology, 9*, 751–780.

Orobio de Castro, B., Veerman, J. W., Koops, W., Bosch, J. D., & Monshouwer, H. J. (2002). Hostile attribution of intent and aggressive behavior: A meta-analysis. *Child-Development, 73*, 916–934.

Patchin, J. W., & Hinduja, S. (2006). Bullies move beyond the schoolyard: A preliminary look at cyberbullying. *Youth Violence and Juvenile Justice, 4*, 148–169.

Patchin, J. W., & Hinduja, S. (2015). Measuring cyberbullying: Implications for research. *Aggression and Violent Behvaior, 23*, 69–740.

Pedersen, S. (2013). UK young adults' safety awareness online—Is it a 'girl' thing? *Journal of Youth Studies, 16*, 404–419.

Pieschl, S., Kuhlmann, C., & Prosch, T. (2015). Beware of publicity! Perceived distress of negative cyber incidents and implications for defining cyberbullying. *Journal of School Violence, 14*, 111–132.

Pyzalski, J. (2012). From cyberbullying to electronic aggression: Typology of the phenomenon. *Emotional and Behavioural Difficulties, 17*, 305–317.

Rafferty, R., & Vander Ven, T. (2014). "I hate everything about you": A qualitative examination of cyberbullying and on-line aggression in a college sample. *Deviant Behavior, 35*, 364–377.

Raskauskas, J., & Stoltz, A. D. (2007). Involvement in traditional and electronic bullying among adolescents. *Developmental Psychology, 43*, 564–575.

Rivers, I. (2013). What to measure? In S. Bauman, D. Cross, & J. Walker (Eds.), *Principles of cyberbullying research: Definitions, measures, and methodology* (pp. 222–237). New York, NY: Routledge.

Rivers, I., & Smith, P. K. (1994). Types of bullying behaviour and their correlates. *Aggressive Behavior, 20*, 359–368.

Robards, B. (2012). Leaving MySpace, joining Facebook: 'Growing up' on social network sites. *Continuum: Journal of Media & Cultural Studies, 26*, 385–398.

Slonje, R., Smith, P. K., & Frisén, A. (2013). The nature of cyberbullying, and strategies for prevention. *Computers in Human Behavior, 29*, 26–32.

Smith, P. K. (2009). Cyberbullying: Abusive relationships in cyberspace. *Zeitschrift für Psychologie/Journal of Psychology, 217*, 180–181.

Smith, P. K., Kupferberg, A., Mora-Merchan, J. A., Samara, M., Bosley, S., & Osborn, R. (2012). A content analysis of school anti-bullying policies: A follow-up after six years. *Educational Psychology in Practice, 28*, 47–70.

Spears, B., Slee, P., Owens, L., & Johnson, B. (2009). Behind the scenes and screens: Insights into the human dimension of covert and cyberbullying. *Zeitschrift für Psychologie/Journal of Psychology, 217*, 189–196.

Spenser, K. A., & Betts, L. R. (2014, May). "People think it's a harmless joke when really it could be hurting someone": Young people's experiences of cyber bullying. Poster presented at the *British Psychological Society Annual Conference*, International Convention Centre, Birmingham.

Stokes, J. K. (2014). The indecent internet: Resisting unwarranted internet exceptionalism in combating revenge porn. *Berkley Technology Law Journal, 29*, 929–952.

Thomas, H. J., Connor, P., & Scott, J. G. (2015). Integrating traditional bullying and cyberbullying: Challenges of definition and measurement in adolescents—A review. *Education Psychology Review, 27*, 135–152.

Tokunaga, R. S. (2010). Following you home from school: A critical review and synthesis of research on cyberbullying victimization. *Computers in Human Behavior, 26*, 277–287.

Valkenburg, P. M., & Peter, J. (2011). Online communication among adolescents: An integrated model of its attraction, opportunities, and risks. *Journal of Adolescent Health, 48*, 121–127.

Vandebosch, H., & Van Cleemput, K. (2008). Defining cyberbullying: A qualitative research into the perceptions of youngsters. *CyberPsychology & Behavior, 11*, 499–503.

Vandebosch, H., & van Cleemput, K. (2009). Cyberbullying among youngsters: Profiles of bullies and victims. *New Media & Society, 11*, 1349–1371.

Wang, J., Iannotti, R. J., & Luk, J. W. (2012). Patterns of adolescent bullying behaviours: Physical, verbal, exclusion, rumor, and cyber. *Journal of School Psychology, 50*, 521–534.

Wang, J., Iannotti, R. J., & Nansel, T. R. (2009). School bullying among adolescents in the United States: Physical, verbal, relational, and cyber. *Journal of Adolescent Health, 45*, 368–375.

Wegge, D., Vandebosch, H., & Eggermont, S. (2014). Who bullies whom online: A social network analysis of cyberbullying in a school context. *Communications, 39*, 415–433.

Whittaker, E., & Kowalski, R. M. (2015). Cyberbullying via social media. *Journal of School Violence, 14*, 11–29.

Willard, N. E. (2007). *Cyberbullying and cyberthreats: Responding to the challenge of online social aggression, threats, and distress.* Champaign, IL: Research Press.

CHAPTER 3

The Unique Nature of Cyberbullying

Abstract Despite some researchers arguing that cyberbullying is an extension of face-to-face bullying (e.g., Olweus, *Annual Review of Clinical Psychology* 9:751–780, 2013), there is growing evidence that cyberbullying represents a unique form of bullying. Together, the digital world, the nature of the power dynamic between the target and perpetrator, the many ways that cyberbullying acts can be repeated, the potential anonymity of the perpetrator, and the relentless nature of cyberbullying characterise why cyberbullying represents a distinct form of bullying. This chapter will review the unique aspects of cyberbullying.

Keywords Cyberbullying • Power • Repetition • Intent • Anonymity • Legal status

As outlined in the previous chapter, some researchers have argued that cyberbullying represents an extension of face-to-face bullying that uses digital means to bully others (e.g., Olweus, 2013). However, other researchers have argued that cyberbullying represents a unique form of bullying with distinct consequences and, as such, should be assessed separately (e.g., Kubiszewksi, Fontaine, Potard, & Auzoult, 2015; Pieschl, Kuhlmann, & Prosch, 2015). The main rationale for considering cyberbullying as a unique experience, separate from face-to-face bullying,

L.R. Betts, *Cyberbullying*, DOI 10.1057/978-1-137-50009-0_3

is that cyberbullying has many distinct characteristics that extend above and beyond those associated with face-to-face bullying. Further, whilst society has typically moved away from the idea that experiencing face-to-face bullying is part of growing up, some have argued that cyberbullying is less serious than face-to-face bullying because there is no physical damage to the target (Anderson & Strum, 2007). The purpose of this chapter is to outline some of the current debates concerning the unique nature of cyberbullying. In particular, the chapter will focus on the nature of the digital world, the power dynamic between the target and perpetrator, the repetition of the acts, anonymity, and the potential relentless nature of cyberbullying. Finally, the chapter will introduce the roles associated with cyberbullying and the complexity of the legal issues associated with cyberbullying.

3.1   THE DIGITAL WORLD

The digital world is a liberating environment for young people (Erdur-Baker, 2010). In the digital world, young people have unprecedented opportunities to express their identities. Similar to face-to-face interactions, the digital world is one where there are also emerging norms that govern interactions and acceptable technology use. Further, these norms are often different to those in the face-to-face environment (Runions, Shapka, Dooley, & Modecki, 2013). Moreover, compared to the school environment, where the majority of face-to-face bullying occurs, the digital world has a number of unique characteristics that impact on experiences of cyberbullying. For example, digital technology use can be private and unlimited and, as such, cyberbullying can rapidly spread, be secret, and be easily preserved (Li, 2006).

Another distinct characteristic of the digital environment, compared to the face-to-face world, is the removal of geographical constraints. Specifically, digital technology has made it possible for perpetrators of cyberbullying to target a large number of people with relative ease that are not confined or constrained by geographical limitations (Surgarman & Willoughby, 2013). In other words, digital technology means that cyberbullying can occur without the target and perpetrator being in the same physical environment. This means that, compared to face-to-face bullying, potentially there are both limitless perpetrators and targets. Also, compared to the face-to-face world, the digital world is less rule-bound and the norms of social interactions are less restrictive. Consequently, the digital world provides young people with a greater opportunity to present different versions of themselves and to more openly speak their mind (Alvarez, 2012), in a way that many may feel uncomfortable doing so in the 'real' world.

One theoretical explanation that accounts for why individuals feel less constrained in the digital world is the online disinhibition effect (Barlett, Gentile, & Chew, 2014). The online disinhibition effect occurs when individuals believe that how they behave online is dissociated from their actions in face-to-face settings. In addition to the behavioural dissociation, individuals also experience cognitive dissociation in terms of their thought processes. Together these dissociations result in changes such that the cognitive processes designed to mediate behavioural and moral engagement, when interacting in social situations, are not applied to the virtual world. Ultimately, it is this dissociation that has been proposed as the underlying reason why individuals engage in more extreme bullying behaviours when engaging in cyberbullying than in face-to-face bullying (Bauman & Yoon, 2014).

Empirical evidence for the online disinhibition effect has recently been provided by Schultze-Krumbholz et al. (2015) using latent class analysis. Latent class analysis is a technique that uses a person-centred approach, rather than the typical variable-centred approach in statistical analyses, and can be used to identify profiles of individuals' experiences (Betts & Houston, 2012). The analysis undertaken by Schultze-Krumbholz et al. included 6260 young people, recruited from 6 European countries. The researchers identified three distinct classes of cyberbullying experiences: non-involved, bully/victims, and perpetrator with mild victimisation. The bully/victim group were more likely to report experiencing verbal cyberbullying and engaging in cyberbullying and relational cyberbullying. The perpetrator with mild victimisation group reported engaging in high levels of cyberbullying with the most frequent acts being verbal threats, stealing, and altering personal information. This group also experienced relatively low levels of cyberbullying compared to the amount of cyberbullying they engaged in. In comparison, four groups emerged for face-to-face bullying: non-involved, bully/victim, perpetrator, and bully/victim behaviour with a focus on victimisation. The bully/victim group was likely to experience high levels of verbal bullying and engage in high levels of relational bullying. The perpetrator group was engaged in high levels of physical, verbal, and relational bullying, and experienced comparatively low levels of bullying. Membership to the bully/victim behaviour with a focus on victimisation group was typified by experiencing high levels of verbal, relational, and physical bullying. In addition to providing empirical evidence young people's experiences of face-to-face bullying and cyberbullying are different, the research by Schultze-Krumbholz et al. also provide empirical evidence of the social disinhibition effect in cyberbullying. Specifically, the lack of a clearly defined target group for cyberbullying reflects the online disinhibition effect and suggests that targets of cyberbullying may use digital technology to 'get their own back' on their perpetrators, and, as such, targets of cyberbullying do not constitute a separate group.

Young people also believe that cyberspace is an impersonal environment which means that they can say what they want (Li, 2006). Linked to the nature of social disinhibition in the digital world, researchers have argued that behaviour can change in other ways. For example, a lack of social censorship when engaging in online interactions (Bussey, Fitzpatrick, & Raman, 2015) because many of the social restraints that likely come in to play in face-to-face bullying do not do so in cyberbullying. In face-to-face bullying, targets and perpetrators are able to interpret non-verbal cues associated with the actions and, depending on the context, immediately have access to the responses of witnesses. Consequently, because of this dearth of social restraints in the digital world, Bussey et al. argue that personal regulation factors, such as morality, are more important in the digital world.

Morals are those guiding principles that individuals draw on when they interact with others to determine what constitutes appropriate behaviour. However, individuals have the ability to regulate the perceived importance of their morals in a given situation. Consequently, the process of moral disengagement enables those young people who engage in cyberbullying to selectively disengage or suspend their moral beliefs during a particular episode of cyberbullying. Therefore, for perpetrators engaging in cyberbullying, their actions do not cause internal conflict, psychological distress, or loss of self-regard. Resultantly, because of this perceived lack of consequences, individuals may be more likely to engage in behaviours that they would not usually do so. In other words, as Festl and Quandt (2013) propose, the boundaries of socially acceptable behaviour change when individuals interact online and this, in turn, may facilitate and perpetuate cyberbullying. Associated with the changes in morals in cyberspace, the digital world also impacts on empathy. Specifically, it has been argued by Mason (2008) that by its very nature, the digital world does not promote empathy development or provide validation of empathic acts, and, as such, young people may be more likely to engage in cyberbullying because they do not feel a sense of empathy towards the target.

The time displacement hypothesis (Espinosa & Clemente, 2013) offers another theoretical perspective as to how the digital world can influence, and impact on, young people's cyberbullying experiences. Espinosa and Clemente argue that the time that young people spend online detracts from time spent engaging in other activities which may impact on their face-to-face socialisation opportunities. Consequently, because young people are spending increasing amounts of time in the digital world, this has the unintended consequence of limiting their face-to-face social interactions. By limiting their face-to-face social interactions this may, in turn, limit young people's opportunities to develop cognitive and social skills that are refined through such social interactions. There is also empirical evidence that young people who spend greater amounts of time online are more likely to be a target and perpetrator of cyberbullying (Didden et al., 2009).

Another aspect of the digital world that has been associated with cyberbullying is that because of the many, and varied, forms of technology currently used by young people, they can feel bombarded when they experience cyberbullying in a way that is distinct to face-to-face bullying (Darden, 2009). Specifically, because cyberbullying can occur through text messages, voice mails, emails, chatrooms, social networking sites, and instant messengers, there are potentially more avenues to target young people than in face-to-face bullying. Therefore, as Keith and Martin (2005) have argued, digital technology has made it easier for perpetrators to reach their targets. However, because of the many forms of cyberbullying, it is possible for young people to document and record what has happened to them when they experience cyberbullying which may not always be possible in face-to-face situations (Darden, 2009).

In summary, the digital world has a number of unique characteristics that means that the nature of the environment is likely to impact on young people's experiences of cyberbullying. These characteristics are likely to particularly impact on both the targets and the perpetrators cyberbullying. However, because of the nature of the digital world compared to the 'real' world, anyone can become a target of cyberbullying, because unlike face-to-face bullying, cyberbullying often does not occur because of a characteristic of the individual (Beale & Hall, 2007). The remaining sections of this chapter will consider more specific differences with regard to face-to-face bullying and cyberbullying, some of which result from the nature of the digital technology.

3.2   REPETITION

One of the most frequently debated aspects of cyberbullying is the nature of repetition. Whilst Smith (2004) questioned whether an act needed to be repeated more than once over an unlimited time frame or whether the time frame needed to be specified to be conceptualised as face-to-face bullying, there is a consensus in the literature that definitions of face-to-face bullying must include reference to repetition. As discussed in Chap. 2, some definitions of cyberbullying dictate that for a behaviour to be conceptualised as cyberbullying, similar to face-to-face bullying, the behaviour must be repeated. However, repetition in cyberbullying can take different forms. For example, a target may experience repeated acts from the same perpetrator, a single act could be viewed by many different audiences on repeated occasions, or the same one off act could be perpetuated by an individual who was not the original perpetrator. Consequently, whilst these acts constitute subtly different forms of repetition, they can still be considered to be repetition in the context of cyberbullying (Slonje, Smith, & Frisén, 2013).

An example of how a single act that is repeated many times can constitute cyberbullying is provided by the well-documented case of Ghyslain Raza. Ghyslain filmed himself in 2002 pretending to be a character out of the film *Star Wars*. This private footage was then made available online and viewed over billion times and led to him being nicknamed the *Star Wars Kid*. Ten years later, Ghyslain talked about the negative impact that this viral video has had on his life, including many people calling for him to commit suicide (Anon, 2013). Despite Ghyslain only appearing on a single video, which was made available once, because the video has been viewed so many times, this experience can be regarded as cyberbullying. Dooley, Pyżalski, and Cross (2009) argue that when a single act is viewed by different and multiple audiences with the intent to ridicule the target, this has the effect of the target experiencing repeated humiliation because although the act is not repeated the negative experience associated with it is.

Due to the ambiguities surrounding whether an act needs to be repeated to be considered cyberbullying or whether the repetition is associated with the audience, a number of researchers have challenged how repetition is thought about in the context of cyberbullying. For example, Dooley et al. (2009) argue that repetition of cyberbullying may also be associated with the content of the message rather than as a feature of the perpetrators' actions or intentions such that if the message is publically available, there is the potential of the consequences of it being relived indefinitely. More recently, Rodkin and Fischer (2012) argue that repetition should not be considered a definitional component of cyberbullying but rather a way to work out how serious an episode of cyberbullying is. Specifically, a single act viewed by a potentially growing and unlimited audience may be regarded as having a greater impact than a few repeated acts limited to exchanges simply between the target and the perpetrator.

3.3   AUDIENCE AND VISIBILITY OF CYBERBULLYING

The audience of cyberbullying, and consequently the scope of actions, are also potentially much greater than face-to-face bullying (Holladay, 2011; Tokunaga, 2010). With face-to-face bullying, the likely audience have to be in the same physical space as the perpetrator and the target at the time when the bullying episode occurs to witness it first-hand. However, with the advances in technology, these space and time constraints are removed for cyberbullying. In particular, cyberbullying can be regarded as having a potentially global audience because of the lack of geographical constraints associated with public acts in the digital world (Butler, Kift, & Campbell, 2009). The role of the global audience is crucial: Perpetrators need an audience in order to maximise the impact of their actions on the target (Long, 2008).

The potential scale and scope of the audience of cyberbullying prompted Huang and Chou (2010) to state that the 'maelstrom of cyberbullying can spread quickly and is almost unstoppable' (p. 1582). Consequently, when compared to face-to-face bullying, cyberbullying has the potential to lead to much greater humiliation of the target because the act can be seen by many more people than face-to-face bullying, especially when the act is carried out via social networking sites (Kernaghan & Elwood, 2013). Further, whilst with face-to-face bullying individuals may hear second-hand about a bullying episode, because of the permanence and history associated with some forms of technology, cyberbullying episodes can be witnessed following a significant delay from when the event occurred.

The role of the audience has also been implicated as an antecedent for why individuals engage in cyberbullying. For example, Rafferty and Vander Ven (2014) reported that 13.6% of their sample of undergraduates had experienced 'cyber sanctioning'. Due to the visibility, and potentially wide ranging audience, 'cyber sanctioning' involves an individual feeling pressured to change their behaviour because of their peers. This type of activity tends to occur between individuals who know each other in the face-to-face world, as well as the virtual world. The underlying reasons for this pressure were attributed to performing badly on a task such as in a gaming context, breaking a social norm, or violating a dating norm and the behaviour would take the form of insults or name-calling through social media sites. Consequently, 'cyber sanctioning' was seen as both a mechanism to control undesirable behaviour and a way to exert informal social control. However, there was also an element of inducing shame in the individual who had engaged in the inappropriate behaviour.

The role of others in the digital world is also potentially influenced by the nature of the technology. Researchers such as Salmivalli (2014) have argued that witnesses of face-to-face bullying play an important role in moderating the behaviour of those who engage in bullying episodes. Many bystanders may reinforce the behaviour of the perpetrator through their verbal or non-verbal behaviours, some may join in with the perpetrator, or others who remain silent may inadvertently reinforce the perpetrators' actions. On the other hand, some bystanders may support and defend the target against the perpetrator or make it clear to the perpetrator that their behaviour is not appropriate. As well as potentially limiting the perpetrators' actions, these bystanders who intervene to support the target also provide a protective buffer for the target from some of the negative adjustment consequences associated with experiencing bullying (Salmivalli, 2014). However, in the virtual world, the role of bystanders is different (Mehari, Farrell, & Le, 2014). Specifically, because the bystanders are often not visible in the digital world, their effectiveness is likely to be reduced because others cannot actively witness their disapproval of the cyberbullying behaviour.

Aligned to the audience, and also drawing on aspects of repetition, is the extent to which acts of cyberbullying can be considered to be permanent (Bauman & Yoon, 2014). Compared to face-to-face bullying episodes which may have faded from memory with time, depending on the media used to target an individual, there may be a permanent record of the cyberbullying episode. Although young people can take steps to try to remove the records of cyberbullying such as asking for content to be removed either by moderators or under the new 'right to be forgotten' law introduced across Europe. As Rosen (2012) argues, the right to be forgotten means that people have the potential to avoid and delete things that have appeared about them in the past. However, the success of such requests is often limited or there is a time lag between the request being made and action being taken. Together, this may explain why young people believe that the potential visibility of cyberbullying to a wider audience means that cyberbullying is regarded as more harmful and with greater potential consequences than face-to-face bullying (Bryce & Fraser, 2013).

In addition to the comparable permanence of the record of cyberbullying, and the relatively large audience, with cyberbullying, there is also the possibility of the target repeatedly viewing the same bullying episode (Srivastava, Gamble, & Boey, 2013). Young people's ability to review and relive cyberbullying episodes was highlighted by teachers through a series of focus groups exploring perceptions of cyberbullying and digital technology (Betts & Spenser, 2015). Specifically, the teachers discussed how young people would often repeatedly view cyberbullying episodes as a mechanism to punish themselves and, this, in turn, would negatively impact on their well-being. This ability to review and replay cyberbullying by the target was also highlighted as a unique characteristic of cyberbullying because, unlike many cases of face-to-face bullying, there was physical evidence of what the target had experienced.

3.4   POWER

The nature of the power imbalance between the target and the perpetrator in cyberbullying is also potentially different from that in face-to-face bullying. Indeed, some researchers have argued that the power imbalance does not exist in cyberbullying because power and status are neutralised by technology (e.g., Lapidot-Lefler & Dolev-Cohen, 2015), whereas others argue that the power imbalance is greater because of the anonymity associated with technology (e.g., Raskauskas & Stoltz, 2007). Although Smith (2004) has questioned whether the power imbalance in face-to-face bullying occurs because it is inferred from the perspective of the target(s) or because of characteristics of the perpetrator(s) such as physical strength or number, the nature of the power imbalance in cyberbullying is less resolute. Unlike face-to-face bullying, the power imbalance in cyberbullying is not necessarily aligned to physical strength but rather technological knowledge and anonymity (Slonje et al., 2013). In other words, the power imbalance in cyberbullying can be considered to be reflective of the lack of power that the target has rather than a characteristic of the perpetrator per se (Dooley et al., 2009). The ability for a perpetrator to remain anonymous can influence the power balance between the target and perpetrator such that the perpetrator becomes more powerful, because they are able to hide their identity and foster suspicion as to who they are (Davies, Randall, Ambrose, & Orand, 2014; Patchin & Hinduja, 2006).

The power imbalance in cyberbullying may also occur because of the extent to which targets of cyberbullying may be able to respond to such episodes. Butler et al. (2009) argue that because of the global scope of the potential audience of cyberbullying, this renders the targets of cyberbullying powerless. Specifically, as previously mentioned, young people are often powerless to remove publically available information about them that has occurred as part of cyberbullying episode. In order to remove the material, the young people either have to ask the website owners or moderators to do so, and this may not be a simple process. Aligned to this concept of power is the notion that, compared to face-to-face environments where bullying may occur, there is a relative lack of supervision in the digital world (Patchin & Hinduja, 2006). Typically, when face-to-face bullying occurs at school, there is likely to be either direct supervision or policies concerning how school based bullying should be tackled. Conversely, because of the nature of digital technology, there is much less supervision. Consequently, this lack of supervision potentially empowers perpetrators of cyberbullying to engage in behaviour that may normally be constrained by the rules that govern social interactions.

Power has also been attributed as a motive for why perpetrators engage in cyberbullying. For example, 24.3% undergraduate students reported that the 'power struggle' associated with cyberbullying was one of the reasons for engaging in the behaviour (Rafferty & Vander Ven, 2014). The 'power struggle' was regarded as an attempt to hurt, humiliate, or influence the behaviour of another with the ultimate aim of gaining valued resources. According to the participants, the valued resources ranged from romantic relationships, sex, to performing well in video games. Attacks based on race were also identified as an example of a power struggle by the participants. The most frequent form of power struggle identified by Rafferty and Vander Ven was between individuals who had previously engaged in a romantic relationship. Power struggles aligned to romantic relationships involved previous partners trying to hurt or humiliate their ex-partner or engaging in similar behaviours in an attempt to resume the relationship. Alternatively, the participants reported that the power struggle could be directed at the previous partner's new partner in an attempt to undermine the new relationship.

Although power may be a motive for cyberbullying, there is evidence that the motives of perpetrators of cyberbullying vary according to their goals. Rodkin and Fischer (2012) propose two types of cyberbullies: socially integrated and marginalised bullies. Socially integrated bullies may engage in cyberbullying acts because by doing so, it gives them the power to avoid becoming the target of other perpetrators. Conversely, marginalised bullies may engage in cyberbullying as a way to gain power because they have self-regulation difficulties, impulse control challenges, or the desire to gain a social status that they cannot achieve through other mechanisms. Consequently, Rodkin and Fischer argue that whilst socially integrated bullies' behaviour can be seen as adaptive and functional, the behaviour of marginalised bullies is maladaptive and dysfunctional.

The conceptualisations of power discussed in this part of the chapter are very different to the conceptualisations of power that have been discussed with regard to face-to-face bullying which have been more inclined to differences in physical strengthen (Smith, 2004). Consequently, because the power imbalance in cyberbullying relies less on physical attributes, there is growing evidence that many targets of face-to-face bullying are using cyberbullying as a mechanism to retaliate against their perpetrator (König, Gollwitzer, & Steffgen, 2010). It has also been proposed that the anonymity associated with cyberbullying and the potentially large audience (both discussed elsewhere in this chapter) are the factors that most likely influence the power imbalance in cyberbullying (Thomas, Connor, & Scott, 2015). An alternative account of the power imbalance in cyberbullying was proposed by Vandebosch and Van Cleemput (2008) who argued that the power imbalance could be based on a 'real life' characteristic, such as age or physical strength, or an information and communication technology (ICT) characteristic such as technological knowledge or anonymity.

Irrespective of how researchers conceptualise the power imbalance in cyberbullying, when there is a perceived imbalance of power between the target and perpetrator, young people rate the cyberbullying episode more negatively (Talwar, Gomez-Garibello, & Sharriff, 2014). Talwar et al. gave participants hypothetical moral vignettes that manipulated power across situations and participants had to report whether they thought the act constituted cyberbullying. The participants more readily reported that scenarios, including an imbalance of power, constituted cyberbullying. Further, when the imbalance of power was evident, the actions of the perpetrator were rated more negatively than when there was no information concerning the power imbalance. Therefore, it may be that the power imbalance between perpetrator and target of cyberbullying does not have to be quantifiable by witnesses but rather something that is inferred by the target.

3.5   ANONYMITY

In most direct cases of face-to-face bullying, the target is likely to be able to identify the perpetrator. However, with cyberbullying, the true identity of the perpetrator may be harder to accurately determine. Digital technology enables individuals to feel anonymous because they can either hide or manipulate their true identity. Consequently, this perceived sense of anonymity has prompted some authors to argue that the Internet affords cyberbullying perpetrators with more freedom to act (Hinduja & Patchin, 2008). In support of this proposition, Aricak et al. (2008) reported that 59.5% of their sample disclosed that they would say things online that they would not say in a face-to-face setting.

The anonymity of the perpetrator can impact on cyberbullying for a number of reasons. First, as previously discussed, by hiding their true identity, it affords the perpetrator more power over the target. Second, the anonymity means that the perpetrator is unlikely to be easily identified so they may believe that their actions are less likely to be judged by those who know them. Third, anonymity can also act at the level of the perpetrator such that they are anonymous to the consequences of their actions because they are not in same physical space as their target. Fourth, anonymity may also enhance the level of fear and confusion that a target experiences, because the perpetrator could be a friend, a fellow group member, or someone truly unknown (Anderson & Strum, 2007).

Focusing on the role of anonymity as a mechanism to modify the perpetrators' actions, Huang and Chou (2010) argue that the potential anonymity in the digital world also allows individuals to engage in behaviour that does not threaten themselves. Specifically, because individuals are able to hide their true identity, then they feel that they are less likely to be judged by others and, as such, may be motivated to engage in acts that they know would be perceived negatively by others in the social world. Linked to this freedom to act, because of a lack of social constraints, young people have reported that those who engage in cyberbullying do so because their identity is hidden, and this empowers them (Mishna, Schwan, Lefebvre, Bhole, & Johnston, 2014). This sense of empowerment is likely to perpetuate an individual's cyberbullying behaviour and has been linked to the perception that using technology to bully means that the perpetrators feel that they are invisible (Slonje & Smith, 2008). Further, this anonymity also reduces the perpetrators' fear of being caught and punished for their actions which may encourage them to engage in more extreme behaviour (Beale & Hall, 2007).

As well as impacting on the behaviour that individuals may engage in, the anonymity afforded by digital technology is also likely to influence how individuals perceive cyberbullying. In comparison to the face-to-face world where the perpetrator is often known, and in some cases visible, the potential anonymity afforded to perpetrators in the digital world influences their perceptions of cyberbullying. For example, Barlett and Gentile (2012) provided empirical evidence that involvement in cyberbullying was predicted both by positive attitudes towards cyberbullying and perceptions of anonymity such that when individuals were aware of anonymity they were more likely to engage in cyberbullying.

There are a number of mechanisms that account for the role of anonymity in cyberbullying. Dehue, Bolman, and Völlink (2008) argue that anonymity in cyberbullying can be linked to the social identity model of deindividuation. Specifically, because the target and their reactions to the cyberbullying episode remain anonymous to the perpetrator, the perpetrator can disengage from the potential distress that they are causing and, as such, continue their behaviour. Therefore, the target of the cyberbullying is not regarded as an individual with common humanity but rather the perpetrator is able to down play the targets' feelings which, in the perpetrators' mind, would facilitate a sense of legitimacy for their actions.

Another way in which anonymity can operate with regards to cyberbullying is that in the virtual world the target and perpetrator do not have to have previously had a relationship (Barlett, 2015). Therefore, because the target is relatively unknown to the perpetrator (especially when compared to face-to-face bullying), the perpetrator may engage in more extreme forms of cyberbullying because they do feel constrained by the previous nature of their relationship with the target. Further, this lack of a shared history may also further promote the sense of deindividuation that the perpetrator experiences.

Barlett (2015) also argues that anonymity can also arise because in some cases, there may be no physical signs that cyberbullying has occurred. Specifically, depending on the mechanism used to cyberbully, there may not be a history. For example, if a message was sent through an application such as SnapChat which only displays messages for a short period of term, unless the target had taken steps to capture the image, then there would be no physical record of the incident. Linked to this lack of physical evidence is the perception that because cyberbullying acts can be anonymous, the perpetrator often believes that they are less likely to get caught and are less likely to experience punishment online than they would do if they engaged in face-to-face bullying (Barlett et al., 2014).

There are two well-documented cases from America that highlight the role attributed to anonymity and identity manipulation in cyberbullying. The first case is Rachael Neblett. Rachael, a frequent user of MySpace, began receiving malicious messages from an anonymous MySpace user (Moreno, 2011c). The messages contained personal information which resulted in Rachael feeling like she was constantly being watched. Following a death threat from an anonymous MySpace user, Rachael committed suicide. The second of these cases is that of Megan Meier. Megan was 13 when she developed a relationship with Josh Evans through MySpace (Moreno, 2011d). However, Josh's profile had been created by the mother of one of Megan's schoolmates. Once Josh had befriended Megan, the nature of their communication changed and became malicious with Josh posting negative comments about Megan on online forums. After the relationship between Megan and Josh disintegrated further, Megan subsequently committed suicide. Megan's suicide was partly attributed to her experiences of cyberbullying. Both Rachael's and Megan's experiences of cyberbullying from either anonymous or fake profiles respectively, underscores the potentially negative and extreme consequences of experiencing cyberbullying (which are further discussed in Chap. 5).

Alongside influencing the dynamic between the perpetrator and the target, the anonymity associated with cyberbullying influences the actions of the larger social group. Specifically, anonymity impacts on whether individuals who witness cyberbullying intervene. There is some evidence that because individuals are anonymous in the virtual world, they are less likely to intervene in cyberbullying episodes because of diffusion of responsibility occurs (Burton, Florell, & Wygant, 2013). In other words, young people may be less likely to do something because they believe that someone else will do something about it, because the audience is large and they do not necessarily feel connected with the target of cyberbullying. University students also report that they do not intervene when they witness cyberbullying, because they believe that it is not their responsibility and they did not want to make the situation worse (Gahagan, Vaterlus, & Frost, 2016). Of course, another issue around intervening is that because witnesses may not know who the perpetrator is, they would not know who to direct their attention towards. For a further discussion on issues around interventions in cyberbullying, please see Chap. 6.

Whilst greater anonymity may be associated with increased frequency of cyberbullying (Barlett, 2015), it is important to consider whether individuals can ever be truly anonymous in the digital world. Although users have the ability to create fake profiles and impersonate other users, it is important to remember that ultimately Internet service providers can track users' actions and that computers create a history based on the websites a user visits. Further, despite the issue of anonymity being highlighted by many researchers as a key component of cyberbullying that sets it aside from face-to-face bullying, it is important to note that young people can have different perceptions concerning the role of anonymity. For example, findings from focus groups conducted with young people in the UK suggest that cyberbullying from a known individual in the context of a known network is perceived as more damaging for the target than an anonymous act of cyberbullying (Bryce & Fraser, 2013). Similar findings were reported by Reeckman and Cannard (2009) who suggested that the actions of an anonymous perpetrator had less of an impact on the target than a known perpetrator.

3.6   INTENTION

Face-to-face bullying definitions include the need for the act to be intended to cause harm against the target. As with other facets of the definition of cyberbullying, the role of intention is somewhat ambiguous in the context of cyberbullying. For example, intention may relate to the degree to which the perpetrator is aware that they are causing harm to the target (Menesini & Nocentini, 2009). However, how the target interprets the intention of an act is also important because targets may regard an act as cyberbullying that was not necessarily intended to be one (see Chap. 2 Sect. 2.4). Further, the indirect nature of cyberbullying also means that it can be hard to determine intent or whether the act is a reactive action in response to something that has happened to the perpetrator (Menesini & Nocentini, 2009).

3.7   RELENTLESS NATURE OF CYBERBULLYING

Many authors and commentators have discussed the insidious and pervasive nature of cyberbullying (e.g., Srivastava et al., 2013). In particular, compared to face-to-face bullying which young people traditionally knew would likely end for the day when school ended, because of the constant connectedness of society, cyberbullying can be experienced at any time of the day or night. As Davies et al. (2014) note this constant connectedness means that it can be hard for targets of cyberbullying to escape their perpetrator and, as such, may exacerbate the negative consequences associated with cyberbullying for the target. Additionally, Mishna, Saini, and Solomon (2009) reported that in focus groups exploring perceptions of cyberbullying, participants discussed how the relentless nature of cyberbullying undermined their sense of security at home. Specifically, as cyberbullying can occur at any time because of the nature of technology, cyberbullying was regarded by the participants as something that was non-stop and particularly invasive in targets' lives compared to face-to-face bullying. Further, participants thought that the home environment which had traditionally been regarded as a 'safe space' from face-to-face bullying was no longer regarded as such because cyberbullying could occur at any time during the day. Similarly, the constant connectiveness of young people has been recognised by teachers as a source of anxiety with regard to cyberbullying (Betts & Spenser, 2015). Teachers argued that young people were more fearful of the prospect of receiving an episode of cyberbullying rather than the content of the message they received.

Aliened to the relentless nature of cyberbullying is the lack of social cues. Specifically, in face-to-face bullying, both the target and the perpetrator are able to distinguish social cues from the other (Kite, Gable, & Filipelli, 2010). However, these cues which include body posture, speech volume, facial expressions, and levels of engagement are not present in cyberbullying. Therefore, this absence of information may lead the perpetrator to continue their behaviour for longer than they would have done in a face-to-face situation. This lack of time and, to some extent, space restrictions has prompted some researchers to argue that cyberbullying is likely to have more of an adverse effect on young people's well-being (e.g., Bauman & Yoon, 2014). Chapter 5 will discuss greater details of the potential outcomes of experiencing cyberbullying.

3.8   ROLES ASSOCIATED WITH CYBERBULLYING

The face-to-face bullying literature has reported that young people adopt one of six roles when an episode of bullying occurs (Salmivalli, Lagerspetz, Björqvist, Österman, & Kaukiainen, 1996). These roles include victim, bully, reinforcer of the bully, assistant of the bully, defender of the victim, and outsider. However, when considering cyberbullying, it may be more appropriate to adopt a behavioural approach and examine the behaviours/acts that young people experience. Specifically, Law, Shapka, Hymel, Olson, and Waterhouse (2012) reported that Canadian adolescents did not distinguish between the various roles associated with the cyberbullying role but rather the acts themselves.

3.9   COMPLEXITY OF LEGAL STANCE OF CYBERBULLYING

There are also complexities associated with the legal aspects of cyberbullying that are somewhat distinct from face-to-face bullying and, as such, can be considered as one of the unique features of cyberbullying. As with face-to-face bullying, intent is an important aspect of cyberbullying. Smith (2004) argued that in the context of face-to-face bullying, intent may be associated with the intent to carry out an aggressive act without necessarily appreciating the consequences of the action or a greater form of intent to directly harm the target. However, Rodkin and Fischer (2012) suggest that the complexities around intent are greater in cyberbullying. For example, whilst the principle of general intent may be appropriate for cyberbullying because of the possibility that the actions have been undertaken to cause something other than distress in the target, the age of some perpetrators means that they are not aware of the consequences of their actions. Specifically, because young people are still developing, it may be more appropriate to consider specific intent as some young people may be unable to comprehend the consequences of their actions. Rodkin and Fischer argue that this is particularly likely to be the case for those with limited experience of using technology. As well as considering intent from a legal perspective, more recently, Talwar et al. (2014) reported that 12- to 13-year-olds were less able to determine the intent to harm than 15- to 16-year-olds when presented with hypothetical moral vignettes that depicted episodes of cyberbullying, providing empirical evidence of the complexities of intent with regard to cyberbullying.

Associated with the issue of whether intent should be considered at the general or specific level, Rodkin and Fischer (2012) also argue that certain forms of cyberbullying do not fit the general intent principle. For example, a message sent to a third party about the target is more complex, because the target is not the intended recipient of the message but rather the subject of it. This complexity of intent is exemplified in the practice of sharing images of individuals using digital means that are then used beyond their original scope. For a further discussion concerning the legal consequences of cyberbullying, see Chap. 6 Sect. 6.2.

In summary, whilst cyberbullying shares some of the characteristics of face-to-face bullying, there are a number of unique features. Some of the unique features of cyberbullying are associated with the digital environment that it occurs in because of how attitudes and behaviours are modified, considered more liberal, and are not influenced by the norms that govern face-to-face interactions. Further, the nature of technology means that some aspects of cyberbullying can be broadcast to a much larger audience than typical in face-to-face bullying. Similarly, this larger audience is also less likely to be constrained by geography and can also be potentially unlimited in size. Aligned to the concept of unlimited and wide audiences, there is also a greater probability that the cyberbullying event will have a longer history. Targets can also experience cyberbullying at any time of the day, whereas with face-to-face bullying, typically, these experiences end with the school day. Other factors that are also associated with different impacts of cyberbullying include the issues around the anonymity of the perpetrator and the complexities of the power imbalance. Consequently, these unique features have led researchers to explore the different impacts of cyberbullying and prompted some to argue that the consequences of experiencing cyberbullying are greater than those associated with face-to-face bullying, a topic explored in Chap. 5.

References

Alvarez, A. R. G. (2012). "IH8U": Confronting cyberbullying and exploring the use of cybertools in teen dating relationships. *Journal of Clinical Psychology: In Session, 68*, 1205–1215.

Anderson, T., & Strum, B. (2007). Cyberbullying from playground to computer. *Young Adult Library Services*, Winter, pp. 24–27.

Anon. (2013). 10 years later 'Star Wars kid' speaks out. Retrieved August 11, 2015,fromhttp://www.macleans.ca/news/canada/10-years-later-the-star-wars-kid-speaks-out/

Aricak, T., Siyahhan, S., Uzunhasanoglu, A., Saribeyoglu, S., Ciplak, S., Yilmaz, N., & Memmedov, C. (2008). Cyberbullying among Turkish adolescents. *CyberPsychology & Behavior, 11*, 253–261.

Barlett, C. P. (2015). Anonymously hurting others online: The effect of anonymity on cyberbullying frequency. *Psychology of Popular Media Culture, 4*, 70–79.

Barlett, C. P., & Gentile, D. A. (2012). Attacking others online: The formation of cyberbullying in late adolescence. *Psychology of Popular Media Culture, 1*, 123–135.

Barlett, C. P., Gentile, D. A., & Chew, C. (2014). Predicting cyberbullying from anonymity. *Psychology of Popular Media Culture*. Advanced online publication.

Bauman, S., & Yoon, J. (2014). This issue: Theories of bullying and cyberbullying. *Theory Into Practice, 53*, 253–256.

Beale, A. V., & Hall, K. R. (2007). Cyberbullying: What school administrators (and parents) can do. *Clearing House, 18*, 8–12.

Betts, L. R., & Houston, J. E. (2012). The effects of cyber bullying on children's school adjustment. In J. Jia (Ed.), *Educational stages and interactive learning: From kindergarten to workplace training* (pp. 209–230). Hershey, PA: IGI Global.

Betts, L. R., & Spenser, K. A. (2015). "A large can of worms": Teachers' perceptions of young people's experiences using technology. *International Journal of Cyber Behavior, Psychology and Learning, 5*, 15–29.

Bryce, J., & Fraser, J. (2013). "It's common sense that it's wrong": Young people's perceptions and experiences of cyberbullying. *Cyberpsychology, Behavior, and Social Networking, 16*, 783–787.

Burton, K., Florell, D., & Wygant, D. B. (2013). The role of peer attachment and normative beliefs about aggression on traditional bullying and cyberbullying. *Psychology in the Schools, 50*, 103–115.

Bussey, K., Fitzpatrick, S., & Raman, A. (2015). The role of moral disengagement and self-efficacy in cyberbullying. *Journal of School Violence, 14*, 30–46.

Butler, D., Kift, S., & Campbell, M. (2009). Cyber bullying in schools and the law: Is there an effective means of addressing the power imbalance? *eLaw Journal: Murdoch University Electronic Journal of Law, 16*, 84–114.

Davies, K., Randall, D. P., Ambrose, A., & Orand, M. (2014). 'I was bullied too': Stories of bullying and coping in an online community. *Information, Communication & Society, 18*, 357–375.

Darden, E. C. (2009, April). The cyber jungle. *American School Board Journal 196*, 54–56.

Dehue, F., Bolman, C., & Völlink, T. (2008). Cyberbullying: Youngsters' experiences and parental perception. *CyberPsychology & Behavior, 11*, 217–223.

Didden, R., Scholte, R. H. J., Korzilius, H., De Moor, J. M. H., Vermeulen, A., O'Reilly, M., … Lancioni, G. E. (2009). Cyberbullying among students with intellectual and developmental disability in special education settings. *Developmental Neurorehabilitation, 12*, 146–151.

Dooley, J. J., Pyżalski, J., & Cross, D. (2009). Cyberbullying versus face-to-face bullying: A theoretical and conceptual review. *Zeitschrift für Psychologie/Journal of Psychology, 217*, 182–188.

Erdur-Baker, Ö. (2010). Cyberbullying and its correlation to traditional bullying, gender and frequent and risky usage on internet-mediated communication tools. *New Media & Society, 12*, 109–125.

Espinosa, P., & Clemente, M. (2013). Self-transcendence and self-oriented perspective as mediators between video game playing and aggressive behaviour in teenagers. *Journal of Community & Applied Social Psychology, 23*, 68–80.

Festl, R., & Quandt, T. (2013). Social relations and cyberbullying: The influence of individual and structural attributes on victimization and perpetration via the internet. *Human Communication Research, 39*, 101–126.

Gahagan, K., Vaterlus, J. M., & Frost, L. R. (2016). College student cyberbullying on social networking sites: Conceptualization, prevalence, and perceived bystander responsibility. *Computers in Human Behavior, 55*, 1097–1105.

Hinduja, S., & Patchin, J. W. (2008). Personal information of adolescents on the Internet: A quantitative content analysis of MySpace. *Journal of Adolescence, 31*, 125–146.

Holladay, J. (2011). Cyberbullying the stakes have never been higher for students or schools. *Teaching Tolerance, 38*, 42–45.

Huang, Y.-Y., & Chou, C. (2010). An analysis of multiple factors of cyberbullying among junior high school students in Taiwan. *Computers in Human Behavior, 26*, 1581–1590.

Keith, S., & Martin, M. E. (2005). Cyber-bullying: Creating a culture of respect in a cyber world. *Reclaiming Children and Youth, 13*, 224–228.

Kernaghan, D., & Elwood, J. (2013). All the (cyber) world's a stage: Framing cyberbullying as a performance. *Cyberpsychology: Journal of Psychosocial Research on Cyberspace, 7*, 1, article 5.

Kite, S. L., Gable, R., & Filippelli, L. (2010). Assessing middle school students' knowledge of conduct and consequences and their behaviours regarding the use of social networking sites. *The Clearing House, 83*, 158–163.

König, A., Gollwitzer, M., & Steffgen, G. (2010). Cyberbullying as an act of revenge? *Australian Journal of Guidance & Counselling, 20*, 210–224.

Kubiszewksi, V., Fontaine, R., Potard, C., & Auzoult, L. (2015). Does cyberbullying overlap with school bullying when taking modality of involvement into account? *Computers in Human Behavior, 43*, 49–57.

Lapidot-Lefler, N., & Dolev-Cohen, M. (2015). Comparing cyberbullying and school bullying among school students: Prevalence, gender, and grade level differences. *Social Psychology of Education, 18*, 1–6.

Law, D. M., Shapka, J. D., Hymel, S., Olson, B. F., & Waterhouse, T. (2012). The changing face of bullying: An empirical comparison between traditional and internet bullying and victimization. *Computers in Human Behavior, 28*, 226–232.

Li, Q. (2006). Cyberbullying in schools: A research of gender differences. *School Psychology International, 27*, 157–170.

Long, C. (2008). Silencing cyberbullies. *NEA Today*, May, pp. 28–29.

Mason, K. L. (2008). Cyberbullying: A preliminary assessment for school personnel. *Psychology in the Schools, 45*, 323–348.

Mehari, K. R., Farrell, A. D., & Le, A.-T. H. (2014). Cyberbullying among adolescents: Measures in search of a construct. *Psychology of Violence, 4*, 399–415.

Menesini, E., & Nocentini, A. (2009). Cyberbullying definition and measurement: Some critical considerations. *Zeitschrift für Psychologie/Journal of Psychology, 217*, 230–232.

Mishna, F., Saini, M., & Solomon, S. (2009). Ongoing and online: Children and youth's perceptions of cyber bullying. *Children and Youth Services Review, 31*, 1222–1228.

Mishna, F., Schwan, K. J., Lefebvre, R., Bhole, P., & Johnston, D. (2014). Students in distress: Unanticipated findings in a cyber bullying study. *Children and Youth Services Review, 44*, 341–348.

Moreno, G. (2011c). Cases of victimization Case 5: Rachael Neblett (Kentucky, 2006). *Preventing School Failure, 55*, 101.

Moreno, G. (2011d). Cases of victimization Case 1: Megan Meier (Missouri, 2006). *Preventing School Failure, 55*, 70.

Olweus, D. (2013). School bullying: Development and some important challenges. *Annual Review of Clinical Psychology, 9*, 751–780.

Patchin, J. W., & Hinduja, S. (2006). Bullies move beyond the schoolyard: A preliminary look at cyberbullying. *Youth Violence and Juvenile Justice, 4*, 148–169.

Pieschl, S., Kuhlmann, C., & Prosch, T. (2015). Beware of publicity! Perceived distress of negative cyber incidents and implications for defining cyberbullying. *Journal of School Violence, 14*, 111–132.

Rafferty, R., & Vander Ven, T. (2014). "I hate everything about you": A qualitative examination of cyberbullying and on-line aggression in a college sample. *Deviant Behavior, 35*, 364–377.

Raskauskas, J., & Stoltz, A. D. (2007). Involvement in traditional and electronic bullying among adolescents. *Developmental Psychology, 43*, 564–575.

Reeckman, B., & Cannard, L. (2009). Cyberbullying: A TAFE perspective. *Youth Studies Australia, 28*, 41–49.

Rodkin, P. C., & Fischer, K. (2012). Cyberbullying from psychological and legal perspectives. *Missouri Law Review, 77*, 619–640.

Rosen, J. (2012). The right to be forgotten. *Stanford Law Review Online, 64*, 88–92.

Runions, K., Shapka, J. D., Dooley, J., & Modecki, K. (2013). Cyber-aggression and victimization and social information processing: Integrating the medium and the message. *Psychology of Violence, 3*, 9–26.

Salmivalli, C. (2014). Participant roles in bullying: How can peer bystanders be utilized in interventions. *Theory Into Practice, 53,* 286–292.

Salmivalli, C., Lagerspetz, K., Björqvist, K., Österman, K., & Kaukiainen, A. (1996). Bullying as a group process: Participant roles and their relations to social status within the group. *Aggressive Behavior, 22,* 1–15.

Schultze-Krumbholz, A., Göbel, K., Scheithauer, H., Brighi, A., Guarini, A., ... Smith, P. K. (2015). A comparison of classification approaches for cyberbulling and traditional bullying using data from six European countries. *Journal of School Violence, 14,* 47–65.

Slonje, R., & Smith, P. K. (2008). Cyberbullying: Another main type of bullying? *Scandinavian Journal of Psychology, 49,* 147–154.

Slonje, R., Smith, P. K., & Frisén, A. (2013). The nature of cyberbullying, and strategies for prevention. *Computers in Human Behavior, 29,* 26–32.

Smith, P. K. (2004). Bullying: Recent developments. *Child and Adolescent Mental Health, 9,* 98–103.

Srivastava, A., Gamble, R., & Boey, J. (2013). Cyberbullying in Australia: Clarifying the problem, considering the solutions. *International Journal of Children's Rights, 21,* 25–45.

Surgarman, D. B., & Willoughby, T. (2013). Technology and violence: Conceptual issues raised by the rapidly changing social environment. *Psychology of Violence, 3,* 1–8.

Talwar, V., Gomez-Garibello, C., & Shariff, S. (2014). Adolescents' moral evaluations and ratings of cyberbullying: The effect of veracity and intentionality behind the event. *Computers in Human Behavior, 36,* 122–128.

Thomas, H. J., Connor, P., & Scott, J. G. (2015). Integrating traditional bullying and cyberbullying: Challenges of definition and measurement in adolescents— A review. *Education Psychology Review, 27,* 135–152.

Tokunaga, R. S. (2010). Following you home from school: A critical review and synthesis of research on cyberbullying victimization. *Computers in Human Behavior, 26,* 277–287.

Vandebosch, H., & Van Cleemput, K. (2008). Defining cyberbullying: A qualitative research into the perceptions of youngsters. *CyberPsychology & Behavior, 11,* 499–503.

CHAPTER 4

Prevalence

Abstract Although the reported prevalence rates of experiencing cyber-bullying as a target tend to converge between 20 and 40%, there is huge variation in the reported prevalence rates of cyberbullying from the perspective of the target, perpetrator, and perpetrator/target. Some of this variation can be accounted for by methodological differences between studies. However, other factors relating to the sample studied such as their age, sex, and nationality may go some way to explain this variation. In addition to presenting a review of the prevalence rates reported in contemporary research, this chapter will also discuss the factors associated with involvement in cyberbullying.

Keywords Cyberbullying • Prevalence • Predictors of cyberbullying • Perpetrator • Target • Target/perpetrator

This chapter will focus on exploring the prevalence rates of cyberbullying, primarily from the perspective of the target and perpetrator, that have been reported in a range of studies conducted with samples recruited from diverse populations. The chapter will begin by arguing why it is important to consider variations in cyberbullying prevalence rates and the implications of such variation for researchers', practitioners', and stakeholders' understanding of cyberbullying. Next, the chapter will provide a comprehensive review of the reported prevalence rates of cyberbullying. The chapter will then turn its attention to some of the likely explanations for this lack of consensus in the prevalence rates of cyberbullying. Specifically, conceptual/methodological issues, sample characteristics, and the country of study will be discussed with regard to offering potential explanations for the reported variation in the prevalence rates of cyberbullying. Finally, the chapter will also review the literature that has examined the factors that predict involvement in cyberbullying both from the perspective of the target and perpetrator.

4.1   THE IMPORTANCE OF UNDERSTANDING PREVALENCE RATES

According to Smith (2014), understanding the prevalence rates of face-to-face bullying is important for three reasons. First, prevalence rates can be used to raise awareness of the issues surrounding bullying. Second, robust data concerning the prevalence of bullying is needed to enable comparisons between different samples and populations. Third, prevalence rates can be used to draw inferences concerning the effectiveness of anti-bullying interventions. Although Smith was focusing on face-to-face bullying, when he argued about the importance of establishing robust prevalence rates, the same logic can be applied to cyberbullying. Specifically, robust prevalence rates of the roles associated with cyberbullying will (1) raise awareness of the true extent of cyberbullying, (2) enable comparisons between different samples and populations to be made, and (3) allow the effectiveness of anti-cyberbullying interventions to be established (such as those discussed in Chap. 6 Sect. 6.1).

As previously noted, elsewhere in Chaps. 2 and 3, a wide range of studies have been undertaken that examine cyberbullying, and together these studies have used different conceptualisations of cyberbullying and different assessment methods. These studies have yielded reported prevalence rates that range from 1.5% (Ortega, Calmaestra, & Mora-Merchán, 2008) to 72% (Juvonen & Gross, 2008) for experiencing cyberbullying as a target, and 0% (Didden et al., 2009) to 60.4% (Xiao & Wong, 2013) for engaging in cyberbullying as a perpetrator. Prevalence rates for fulfilling the perpetrator/target role in cyberbullying range from 0.6% (Ortega et al., 2008) to 51.7% (Xiao & Wong, 2013). Table 4.1 presents an overview of the reported prevalence rates of cyberbullying as percentages according to participant role as target, perpetrator, and perpetrator/target

Table 4.1 An overview of the reported prevalence rates of cyberbullying according to role as target, perpetrator, and perpetrator/target

Study authors	Age	Country	n	Target	Perpetrator	Perpetrator/target
Accordino and Accordino (2011)	6th grade	USA	124	32%	25%	—
Ackers (2012)	School years 7–9	UK	325	11%	7%	—
Allen (2012)*	9th to 12th grade	USA	807	3.2%	1%	—
Aricak et al. (2008)**	Secondary school	Turkey	296	5.9%	35.7%	23.8%
Bannink et al. (2014)	1st year secondary school	Netherlands	8272	5.1%	—	—
Bauman (2010)	5th to 8th grade	USA	221	3%	1.5%	8.6%
Beran and Li (2005)**	7th to 9th grade	Canada	432	23%	16%	—
Brack and Caltabiano (2014)	17- to 25-year-olds	Australia	164	10%	11%	62%
Brewer and Kerslake (2015)	16- to 18-year-olds	UK	90	16.22%	13.54%	—
Calvete et al. (2010)	12- to 17-year-olds	Spain	1413	44.1%	47.8% (boys) 40.3% (girls)	—
Crosslin and Crosslin (2014)	18- to 53-year-olds	USA	286	32%	16%	—
D'Anotona, Kevorkian, and Russom (2010)	3rd to 5th grade	USA	835	11.4%	—	—
Dehue et al. (2008)**	1st year of secondary school	Netherlands	1211	23%	16%	—
del Barco et al. (2012)*	12- to 16-year-olds	Spain	1700	6%	6.4%	—
Dempsey, Sulkowski, Nichols, and Storch (2009)	11- to 16-year-olds	USA	1665	14%	—	—
Didden et al. (2009	12- to 19-year-olds	Netherlands	114	7%	0%	3%
Erdur-Baker (2010)	14- to 18-year-olds	Turkey	276	32%	26%	—
Fenaughty and Harré (2013)*	12- to 19-year-olds	New Zealand	1668	33%	—	—
Festl and Quandt (2013)	12- to 19-year-olds	Germany	408	4.9%	10.8%	6.4%

(continued)

Table 4.1 (continued)

Study authors	Age	Country	n	Target	Perpetrator	Perpetrator/target
Fletcher et al. (2014)	12- to 13-year-olds	UK	1144	–	14.1%	–
Gahagan, Vaterlus, and Frost (2016)	18- to 25-year-olds	USA	197	18.9%	–	–
Garaigordobil (2015)	12- to 18-year-olds	Spain	3026	30.2%	15.5%	–
Gofin and Avitzour (2012)*	12- to 14-year-olds	Israel	2610	14.4%	8.9%	–
Gomez-Garbiello, Sharriff, McConnel, and Talwar (2012)	12- to 17-year-olds	Canada	115	65%	–	–
Gradinger et al. (2009)	14- to 19-year-olds	Austria	761	7.1%	5.3%	–
Hinduja and Patchin (2008)**	10- to 17-year-olds	Predominately USA	1378	32.7% boys 36.4% girls	18.0% boys 15.6% girls	–
Holfeld and Leadbeater (2015)	5th and 6th grade	Canada	741 (T1) 638 (T2)	22% (T1) 26.8% (T2)	10.2% (T1) 13% (T2)	–
Juvonen and Gross (2008)	12- to 17-year-olds	USA	1454	72%	–	–
Kite, Gable, and Filippelli (2010)	7th and 8th grade	USA	588	10%	10%	–
Kokkinos et al. (2016)	18- to 35-year-olds	Greece	258	–	32.7%	–
Kowalski and Limber (2007)	6th, 7th and 8th grade	USA	3767	11%	4%	7%
Kubiszewksi, Fontaine, Potard, and Auzoult (2015)	10- to 18-year-olds	France	1422	18%	4%	5%
Kwan and Skoric (2013)	13- to 17-year-olds	Singapore	1676	59.4%	56.9%	–
Läftman et al. (2013)*	15- to 18-year-olds	Sweden	22,544	5%	4%	2%
Lam et al. (2013)	13- to 18-year-olds	China	1278	14.4%	2.9%	8.4%

Lemstra, Rogers, Redgate, Garner, and Moracres (2011)*	10- to 16-year-olds	Canada	204	30.4%	—	—
Li (2006)**	7th to 9th grade	Canada	264	25%	17%	—
Li (2007a)**	7th grade	Canada	177	25%	15%	—
Li (2007b)**	7th grade	Canada, China	461	28.9%	17.8%	—
Li (2008)**	11- to 15-year-olds	Canada, China	354	25% (Canada) 33% (China)	15% (Canada) 7% (China)	—
MacDonald and Roberts-Pittman (2010)	University students	USA	439	21.9%	8.6%	—
Marsh, McGee, Nada-Raja, and Williams (2010)	15-year-olds	New Zealand	1165	11%	7%	—
Mesch (2009)	12- to 17-year-olds	USA	935	40%	—	—
Monks, Robinson, and Worlidge (2012)*	7- to 11-year-olds	UK	220	20.5%	5%	—
Moore, Heuber, and Hills (2012)*	Mean age 13	USA	855	20%	14%	—
Olenik-Shemesh et al. (2012)*	13- to 16-year-olds	Israel	242	16.5%	—	—
Olweus (2012a)*	8- to 18-year-olds	USA	450,490	4.5%	2.8%	—
Olweus (2012a)*	9- to 16-year-olds	Norway	9000	3.4%	1.4%	—
Ortega et al. (2008)**	12- to 18-year-olds	Spain	830	1.5%	1.7%	0.6%
Pabian and Vandebosch (2014)	11- to 17-year-olds	Belgium	1606	—	11.7%	—
Patchin and Hinduja (2006)	12- to 18-year-olds	USA, Canada, UK, Australia, other/ unknown	384	29%	11%	—

(continued)

Table 4.1 (continued)

Study authors	Age	Country	n	Target	Perpetrator	Perpetrator/target
Paullet and Pinchot (2014)	18- to 45-year-olds	USA	168	9%	—	—
Pedersen (2013)	10- to 21+ year-olds	UK	226	50%	40%	—
Pelfrey and Weber (2013)*	12- to 18-year-olds	USA	3403	6.8%	10%	—
Popović-Ćitić, Djurić, and Cvetković (2011)*	11- to 15-year-olds	Serbia	387	20%	10%	—
Price, Chin, Higa-McMillan, Kim, and Frueh (2013)	10- to 13-year-olds	Hawaii	211	7%	4%	2%
Pyzalski (2012)*	15-year-olds	Poland	2143	—	4.9%	—
Raskauskas and Stoltz (2007)	13- to 18-year-olds	USA	84	48.8%	21.4%	—
Reeckman and Cannard (2009)	–	Australia	91	8%	11%	49%
Sakellariou, Carroll, and Houghton (2012)*	9- to 18-year-olds	Australia	1530	11.5%	8.5%	—
Schenk and Fremouw (2012)*	18- to 24-year-olds	USA	799	8.6%	—	—
Schneider, O'Donnell, Stueve, and Coulter (2012)*	14- to 18-year-olds	USA	20,406	15.8%	—	—
Schultze-Krumbholz and Scheithauer (2009)	7th, 8th, and 10th grade	Germany	71	15.5%	16.9%	—
Schultze-Krumbholz et al. (2015)[a]	Mean 14.8 years	Poland, Spain, Italy, UK, Germany, and Greece	6260	–	4%	26.1%
Selkie, Kota, Chan, and Moreno (2015)	18- to 25-year-olds	USA	265	17%	3%	7.2%
Smith et al. (2008)**	11- to 16-year-olds	UK	92	22.2%	–	–
Turan, Polat, Karapirli, Uysal, and Turan (2011)	18- to 30-year-olds	Turkey	579	59.8%	–	–

				T1	T2	
Vieno, Gini, and Santinello (2011)*	13- to 16-year-olds	Italy	2667	19.4%	—	—
Wachs (2012)	5th to 10th grade	Germany	517	5.0%	6.2%	4.2%
Wade and Beran (2011)*	10- to 17-year-olds	Canada	529	21.9%	29.7%	—
Walrave and Heirman (2011)*	Mean age 15.1	Belgium	1318	64.3%	39.9%	—
Wang, Iannotti, and Nansel (2009)	6th to 10th grade	USA	7182	9.8%	8.6%	13.6%
Wegge, Vandebosch, and Eggermont (2014)	13- to 14-year-olds	Belgium	1458	14.3%	10%	—
Wensley and Campbell (2012)*	18- to 25-year-olds	Australia	528	11.6%	3.8%	—
West (2015)	16- to 19-year-olds	UK	5690	7.9%	1.9%	—
Whittaker and Kowalski (2015)[b]	18- to 25-year-olds	USA	244	18.2%	12%	—
Whittaker and Kowalski (2015)[c]	18- to 25-year-olds	USA	197	22%	14%	—
Williams and Guerra (2007)**	5th, 8th and 11th grade	USA	3339	—	9.4%	—
Wolak, Mitchell, and Finkelhor, (2007)	10- to 17-year-olds	USA	1500	9%	—	—
Wright, Burnham, Inman, and Ogorchock (2009)	12- to 14-year-olds	USA	450	29.8%	14.9%	—
Xiao and Wong (2013)	University students	Hong Kong	288	71.9%	60.4%	51.7%
Ybarra, Diener-West, and Leaf (2007)	10- to 15-year-olds	USA	1588	34.5%	—	—
Ybarra and Mitchell (2004)**	10- to 17-year-olds	USA	1501	4%	12%	3%
Yilmaz (2011)*	14-year-olds	Turkey	756	17.9%	6.4%	—

Note: T1 = Time 1, T2 = Time 2; [a]perpetrator was with mild victimisation, [b]Study 1, [c]Study 2; studies marked with * appear in Garaigordobil (2015) and ** appear in Calvete et al. (2010)

from the existing published literature (although not all studies assessed all of the roles that individuals fulfil in their assessment of cyberbullying). To facilitate comparisons between the prevalence rates and provide contextualisation for the issues discussed later in this chapter, Table 4.1 also contains details of the sample size, country, and age of the participants.

As evidenced in Table 4.1, there is clear variation in the reported prevalence rates associated with being a target, perpetrator, or perpetrator/target of cyberbullying. For those studies that have classified young people as both perpetrator and target, there is also variation in the extent to which young people fulfil these roles. Interpreting these figures in Table 4.1, according to prevalence rates of cyberbullying, can give readers a very different impression of the magnitude of cyberbullying. For example, as noted in Table 4.1, some of these prevalence rates (e.g., Gomez-Garbiello, Shariff, McConnel, & Talwar, 2012; Kwan & Skoric, 2013; Walrave & Heirman, 2011) support Morgan's (2012) proposition that cyberbullying experiences are pervasive, increasing, and an almost certainty for young people, and that cyberbullying is 'spiralling out of control'. However, viewed differently, some of the figures presented in Table 4.1 from studies with low prevalence rates of experiencing cyberbullying (e.g., Bannink, Broeren, Van de Looij-Jansen, de Waart, & Raat, 2014; del Barco, Castaño, Bullón, & Carroza, 2012; Låftman, Modin, & Östberg, 2013) add support to the argument that cyberbullying is not as serious as some claim, that the scale of phenomenon is misinterpreted, and that it is in fact reducing (Olweus, 2012b). Further, Olweus (2012a) argues that reports of cyberbullying are exaggerated and the claims concerning the prevalence rates lack rigorous scientific support. However, regardless of how you chose to interpret these figures presented in Table 4.1, there are a number of important factors that must be taken into consideration when reviewing prevalence rates of cyberbullying which this chapter will now review.

4.2   Conceptual and Methodological Issues

As discussed in Chap. 2, there is little consensus amongst researchers with regard to how to define cyberbullying. This variation in the conceptualisation and definition of cyberbullying is likely to impact on prevalence rates because of the lack of consensus with regard to what constitutes cyberbullying (Berne et al., 2013). Specifically, if researchers do not implement a consistent definition of cyberbullying across studies, then the variation in prevalence rates can be attributed, in part, to this lack of consistency.

Aside from variations in the definition of cyberbullying that researchers have adopted when assessing cyberbullying, there are a number of pertinent methodological issues associated with the assessment of cyberbullying that may also influence prevalence rates. For example, many of the previous studies assessing cyberbullying have used self-report measures with a self-selected sample (e.g., Hinduja & Patchin, 2008). Consequently, individuals who self-select to participate in such a study and complete these measures may be motivated by their own experiences of cyberbullying to do so, and as such, this could lead to bias reports. Further, as discussed later in this chapter and in Chap. 6, self-reports may cause participants to under-report their experiences of cyberbullying because of the belief that their access to technology may be restricted.

The prevalence rates of cyberbullying are also likely to vary according to whether researchers have assessed cyberbullying as a single item (e.g., Wachs, 2012) or using multiple items (e.g., Menesini, Nocentini, & Calussi, 2011). Single item measures of cyberbullying tend to operate at a more global level and ask young people whether they have ever experienced or engaged in cyberbullying, whereas multiple item measures tend to ask young people about a range of behaviour associated with cyberbullying. Dehue (2013) argues that single item measures can be regarded as subjective, whereas multiple item measures that assess engagement in, and experience of, specific acts of cyberbullying are objective measures. Therefore, participants responding to general questions about whether they are involved in cyberbullying may lead to different results than responding to questions about specific acts or behaviours they have experienced or engaged in when using technology. Specifically, whilst some young people may regard all potential acts or behaviours as cyberbullying, others may view them differently and, as such, respond differently according to the question they were asked.

Dehue (2013) argues that lower prevalence rates of cyberbullying as a perpetrator or a target are likely to be associated with subjective (global single item) measures than objective (multiple item) measures. Further, the use of global measures to assess cyberbullying can lead to an underestimation of the prevalence rates of cyberbullying, because these measures do not take into consideration all of the various behaviours that young people engage in and experience when using technology (Gradinger, Strohmeier, & Spiel, 2010). Empirical evidence of this variation has been provided by Calvete, Orue, Estévez, Villardón, and Padilla (2010) who examined the prevalence of cyberbullying according to specific acts.

Depending on which act the 12- to 17-year-olds were reporting on, the prevalence rates ranged from 8.6% (sending images of classmates performing some kind of sexual behaviour to other people) to 20.2% (deliberately excluding someone from an online group).

Aligned to whether researchers utilise single item or multiple item measures of cyberbullying, the variation in the reported prevalence rates of cyberbullying has also been attributed to the time frame over which young people are asked to report about. For example, some studies have asked young people to report their experiences of cyberbullying over the previous two months (e.g., Menesini et al., 2011), whereas other studies have asked young people to report their involvement in cyberbullying over an unspecified timeframe (e.g., Li, 2006). It is likely that asking young people to report over a greater, and potentially unspecified duration of time, will serve to increase the prevalence of cyberbullying involvement because participants have a greater time frame to draw upon. The impact of changing the duration over which young people are asked to report their experiences of cyberbullying can be empirically evidenced through comparing the prevalence rates of studies that have used different time-frames. For example, Gomez-Garbiello et al. (2012) found that 65% of 12- to 17-year-olds reported that they had experienced cyberbullying at least once. However, when young people were asked about their experiences over the last seven days, the prevalence rates drop dramatically. Lam, Cheng, and Liu (2013) report that 14.4% of their sample were targets of cyberbullying, 2.9% were perpetrators, and 8.4% were perpetrators/targets during the last seven days.

Some researchers have also implemented cut-off points to classify individuals' experiences of cyberbullying as either a perpetrator or target (e.g., Gradinger et al., 2010). Gradinger et al. empirically demonstrated that the prevalence rates of cyberbullying varied in their sample when lenient (i.e., cyberbullying acts occurring at least one or two times during the last couple of months) versus strict (i.e., cyberbullying acts occurring at least two or three times a month) cut-off points were used. When the lenient cut-off point was applied, more perpetrators of cyberbullying were identified for the global measure of cyberbullying compared to the specific measures (6% vs 16% respectively). However, when the stringent cut-off point was applied, fewer perpetrators of cyberbullying were identified using the global measure compared to the specific measures (2% vs 8% respectively). Therefore, Gradinger et al. provided an empirical example, within the same sample of Austrian 14- to 19-year-olds, how the prevalence rates of cyberbullying either as a target or a perpetrator can be manipulated according to the assessment criteria used. Consequently, when interpreting prevalence rates of cyberbullying, it is important to be mindful of the criteria that have been used by the researchers to generate the rates.

Variation in the reported prevalence rates of cyberbullying has also been attributed to how researchers define the media used to experience and engage in cyberbullying. For example, whether young people are asked about their experiences across all media (e.g., Aricak, 2009) or specific media (e.g., Mark & Ratliffe, 2011) can impact on the reported prevalence rates. Whilst asking young people about their experiences across specific media may yield a deeper understanding of cyberbullying according to media type, prevalence rates are likely to be different than when cyberbullying is assessed across all media simultaneously. Moreover, as young people's technology use changes and evolves with the development of new forms of media, asking young people about specific types of media may also reflect the changing importance of a specific technology type rather than cyberbullying per se. As noted elsewhere, trends in young people's technology use and the changing capabilities of technology have impacted on cyberbullying. For example, during the early years of research examining cyberbullying, cyberbullying through a mobile telephone in the form of text messages was distinguished from other forms of cyberbullying via the Internet (Slonje, Smith, & Frisén, 2013). However, Allen (2012) reported that the prevalence rates cyberbullying via text messages was lower than previous studies and argued that this finding reflected changes in how young people are using technology. Of course, this finding may reflect the actual level of cyberbullying within that group of young people, but it may also be indicative of how cyberbullying may be influenced by the popularity of particular forms of technology which may, in turn, impact on the reported prevalence rates.

Another potential reason for the variation in the reported prevalence rates of cyberbullying, as evidenced in Table 4.1, is the likelihood with which young people admit that they involved in cyberbullying. Whilst there may be a number of reasons why young people may under-report their experiences of cyberbullying, there is growing evidence that this is often motivated by the fear that they will have their access to technology restricted if they report that they have experienced cyberbullying (Mishna, Saini, & Solomon, 2009; Thomas, 2006). For a further discussion surrounding the link between cyberbullying reports and access to technology, please see Chap. 6 Sect. 6.1. Young people may also modify their reports of cyberbullying, which, in turn, may impact on prevalence rates, because of social desirability. In some peer groups, it may be acceptable to display very high levels of cyberbullying because of online disinhibition (Barlett, Gentile, & Chew, 2014, see Chap. 3 Sect. 3.1). However, in other contexts, young people may be aware that cyberbullying is something that is regarded by some as socially undesirable (Akbulut & Eristi, 2011) and consequently under-report their involvement.

Together, the studies discussed so far in this chapter provide clear evidence for the argument that the prevalence rates of cyberbullying are likely to vary according to the methodological approaches adopted by researchers. In other words, the specific questions researchers ask young people about their experiences of cyberbullying, and the cyberbullying behaviours they engage in does indeed impact on the reported prevalence rates. Of course, as Olweus (2013) notes, until the variation in the methods used to assess cyberbullying is addressed, comparisons between studies that have used different methods to assess cyberbullying need to be made with caution. Consequently, it may not be appropriate to make comparisons between studies where different methodologies have been used. The next section of this chapter will consider the extent to which characteristics of the research sample may impact on the reported prevalence rates of cyberbullying.

4.3 Sample Characteristics

In addition to the conceptual and methodological factors that may impact on the reported prevalence rates of cyberbullying, other factors that may impact on the prevalence rates are characteristics associated with the sample examined. For example, Olweus (2013) cautions researchers against studying cyberbullying in isolation from face-to-face bullying. Olweus argues that assessing cyberbullying contemporarily with face-to-face bullying enables researchers to contextualise the level of normative aggression within a given sample. In other words, some of the variation in the prevalence rates of cyberbullying could be attributed to differences between samples with regard to the normative nature of aggression for that particular peer group. In support of this proposition, Wright and Li (2013) reported that if young people held beliefs that cyber aggression was normative, this, in turn, predicted higher levels of cyber aggression. Therefore, rather than comparing across studies with regard to cyberbullying, it may be more appropriate to examine prevalence of cyberbullying with samples who share similar characteristics.

In addition to the variation in the norms surrounding appropriate online behaviour and aggression, the age of the sample studied may also account for some of the variation in the prevalence of cyberbullying. Whilst it has been reported by young people that they think that those younger than themselves are more likely to experience cyberbullying (Metwally & Betts, 2015), Ševčíková and Šmahel (2009) provided empirical evidence that those most likely to experience cyberbullying were adolescents and young adults. Further, Ševčíková and Šmahel report that the highest proportion of perpetrators of cyberbullying was young and older adolescents in their study of 12- to 88-year-olds. Similarly, research with 12- to 17-year-olds recruited from Spain suggests that cyberbullying experiences peak around the age of 14 (Ortega et al., 2009), and Kowalski and Limber (2007) report that cyberbullying peaks in 8th graders in America. Therefore, the prevalence rates of cyberbullying could be skewed depending on the age of the samples.

Whilst time spent online may go some way to account for variation in prevalence rates according to age (Kowalski & Limber, 2007), Blakeney (2012) argues that the social dominance theory can offer a theoretical rationale for why cyberbullying may reduce with age. Social dominance theory advocates that within social structures, individuals create hierarchies, with those at the top of the hierarchy controlling the resources available to the rest of the group. Status and dominance are likely gained through bullying behaviours, and, once the hierarchy has established, these bullying behaviours decrease which accounts for the reduction in bullying behaviours with age (Blakeney, 2012). Despite the social dominance theory providing a theoretical explanation for why cyberbullying may reduce with age, other researchers such as Butler, Kift, and Campbell (2009) argue that cyberbullying is more prevalent in older populations. Bulter et al. account for this increase by proposing that young people have grown up with technology, and, as such, communication via technology is becoming increasingly normative which is then placing them in a situation of vulnerability to experience greater levels of cyberbullying with age. Further, older children and adolescents are also likely to be more skilled in their technology use compared to younger children.

There has also been variation in the reported prevalence rates of cyberbullying according to sex as highlighted for some studies in Table 4.1. Some studies have reported that females are more likely to be the targets of cyberbullying than males (e.g., Dehue, Bolman, & Völlink, 2008; Festl & Quandt, 2013; Kowalski & Limber, 2007). Females are also more likely to report more distress when confronted by a cyberbullying episode compared to males (Bauman & Newman, 2013). Conversely, other studies have reported that males are more likely to be the perpetrators of cyberbullying (e.g., Gradinger, Stochmeirer, & Spiel, 2009; Lapidot-Lefler & Dolev-Cohen, 2015). A number of studies have also reported a lack of significant sex differences with regard to who is more likely to be a target cyberbullying (e.g., Hinduja & Patchin, 2008; Juvonen & Gross, 2008; Katzer, Fetchenhauer, & Belschak, 2009)

Some researchers have also argued that time spent online may impact on the prevalence rates of cyberbullying and the likelihood with which an individual is a target or perpetrator of cyberbullying. Specifically, the more time a young person spends online, the potentially greater the risk that they will encounter cyberbullying because of a mere exposure effect. In other words, because some young people spend a large of amount of time using technology by virtue of this technology use, they are likely to experience, and engage in, cyberbullying. Empirical evidence for this claim was provided by Sengupta and Chaudhuri (2011), who found that 12- to 17-year-olds from America who reported that they engaged in low frequency use of social network sites were less likely to experience online harassment. Similarly, Mesch (2009) reported that being a target of cyberbullying was predicted by spending more time using technology, participating in YouTube clips and public chats, and having a social network site profile. Therefore, when comparing the prevalence rates of cyberbullying, it may be prudent to consider the amount of time young people spend using technology, because if the sample comprises a group of very active and frequent technology users, then this may distort the prevalence rates associated with cyberbullying.

4.4   Country of Study

Variation in the reported prevalence rates of cyberbullying can also be attributed to the country the sample was recruited from as Table 4.1 illustrates. For example, in a study of over 16,000 young people recruited from 11 European countries, the reported prevalence rate was 20.6% across the entire sample (Analitis et al., 2009). However, this figure masks nuances in the prevalence rate according to country. When considered according to country, the range of prevalence rates varied from 10.5% for Hungary to 29.6% for the UK. The researchers identified Austria, the Netherlands, Spain, Switzerland, and the UK as countries where cyberbullying prevalence was above the reported average and France, Greece, and Hungary as countries where cyberbullying prevalence was below the reported average. Similar variation in prevalence rates according to European Union countries have been reported for experiences of cyberbullying via mobile telephones in a sample of 9- to 16-year-olds recruited from 25 countries (Görzig & Frumkin, 2013). Young people from Sweden were more likely to experience cyberbullying via mobile telephones compared to the other countries. Young people from Bulgaria and Denmark were least likely to experience cyberbullying via mobile phones compared to those from other countries. More recently, Schultze-Krumbholz et al. (2015) in a study with 6260 young people recruited from Poland, Spain, Italy, the UK, Germany, and Greece reported that Greek participants were more likely to belong to the perpetrator with mild victimisation group than the non-involved group compared to all participants from all of the other countries except Poland. Participants from Germany were significantly less likely to be in the perpetrator with mild victimisation group than the non-involved group compared to all other countries. Finally, participants from Italy were more likely to belong to the perpetrator/target group compared to the non-involved group.

Whilst it remains unclear as to why prevalence rates vary according to the country of study, prevalence rates of cyberbullying may also reflect cross-cultural differences in how cyberbullying is defined. For example, Menesini and Nocentini (2009) argue that samples recruited from different countries often have a different understanding or conceptualisation of cyberbullying. In support of this proposition, Spenser and Betts (2014) found that young people from the UK could readily distinguish between cyberbullying and 'banter'. However, although there is some evidence that young people from America make the distinction between cyberbullying and 'drama' (Allen, 2012), it remains unclear whether young people from other countries make these distinctions.

4.5   FACTORS THAT PREDICT INVOLVEMENT
IN CYBERBULLYING

Related to the prevalence rates of cyberbullying, researchers have also begun to explore the factors that predict involvement in cyberbullying. A range of variables have been explored by researchers to examine what predicts being a target of cyberbullying. These factors have been classified as sociodemographic (including gender and age), psychological (including self-esteem and social anxiety), educational (including academic achievement, experiencing of face-to-face bullying, and experiences at school), family (including parental control), and technological (including frequency of use and risky Internet behaviours, Álvarez-García, Núñez Pérez, Dobarro, Gonález, & Rodríguez Pérez, 2015). In a sample of Spanish 11- to 19-year-olds, Álvarez-García et al. reported that being a target of cyberbullying was predicted by being a target of face-to-face victimisation, engaging in risky technology use, and using technology more frequently. Similarly, problem behaviours, reduced self-esteem, and enhanced depressive symptoms (Modecki, Barber, & Vernon, 2013) and loneliness (Olenik-Shemesh, Heiman, & Eden, 2012) predicted being a target of cyberbullying. Targets of cyberbullying are also more likely to be dependent on the Internet, feel less popular, and engage in more risk taking behaviour (Vandebosch & van Cleemput, 2009). Other risk factors for being a target of cyberbullying include feeling lonely, being unpopular, and having no friends (Wachs, 2012). Young people are also more likely to experience Internet harassment if they experience major depressive symptoms rather than mild or absent depressive symptoms (Ybarra, 2003). University students are also more likely to experience cyberbullying if they have higher interpersonal sensitivity and psychoticism (Aricak, 2009). One reason why anxiety may predispose young people to experiencing cyberbullying as a target is that worrying about others' perceptions of them exacerbates potential vulnerability (Navarro, Yubero, Larrañaga, & Martínez, 2012).

As highlighted elsewhere in this text, time spent online has been identified as a consistent risk factor that impacts on the likelihood that an individual will experience cyberbullying. However, it may be the specific activities that an individual engages in that are a risk factor for experiencing cyberbullying rather than the amount of time per se. For example, Mesch (2009) reported that being a target of cyberbullying was predicted by having an active social network profile and participating in YouTube clips and public chatrooms but not online gaming. Targets of cyberbullying are also more likely to spend time in digital environments that are deemed to be risky such as extremist, pornographic, or hooligan chatrooms (Katzer et al., 2009). Similarly, exposure to media violence is also predictive of involvement in cyberbullying as a perpetrator and target (Fanti, Demetriou, & Hawa, 2012).

Focusing on the perpetrator of cyberbullying, a number of studies have reported a range of factors that predict involvement. For example, those young people who engage in Internet harassment, which has been considered to be a form of cyberbullying, are more likely to report frequent substance use, delinquency, and poor relationships with their parents (Ybarra & Mitchell, 2004). Elevated levels of problem behaviours and depressive mood and reduced levels of self-esteem (Modecki et al., 2013), high levels of aggression (Wang, Iannotti, & Luk, 2012), and lower grades at school (Connell, Schell-Bussey, Pearce, & Negro, 2014) also predict involvement in cyberbullying as a perpetrator. Similarly, for university students, fulfilling the cyberbullying perpetrator role is also predicted by higher levels of phobic anxiety and somatisation psychiatric symptoms (Aricak, 2009) and Internet self-efficacy (Xiao & Wong, 2013). Engaging in cyberbullying through Facebook for male university students from Greece was predicted by spending more time using Facebook and low levels of agreeableness, although similar relationships were not evident for females (Kokkinos, Balzidis, & Xynogala, 2016). Together, these studies suggest that characteristics of the individual as well as their engagement with technology are potential risk factors for becoming a perpetrator of cyberbullying.

Research has also provided examples of where perpetrators and targets of cyberbullying share similar traits and these traits, in turn, predict involvement in cyberbullying. For example, compared to those young people who are not involved in cyberbullying, targets and perpetrators have lower empathy scores and higher relational aggression scores (Schultze-Krumbholz & Scheithauer, 2009). However, there was no significant difference according to involvement in cyberbullying for perspective taking and social intelligence.

The range of factors that are associated with involvement in cyberbullying, either as a perpetrator or target, have been recently summarised by Kowalski, Giumetti, Schroeder, and Lattanner (2014) in their meta-analysis of cyberbullying. Being a target of cyberbullying was predicted by being a target of face-to-face bullying, anger, risky online behaviour, frequency of Internet use, social anxiety, moral disengagement, and hyperactivity. A number of factors were also identified as ones that protected young people from experiencing cyberbullying and these included school safety, school climate, social intelligence, perceived support, and parental monitoring. However, empathy, age, and parental control of technology were identified as not significantly predicting involvement in cyberbullying as a target. Kowalski et al. reported that being a perpetrator of cyberbullying was predicted most strongly by being a target of cyberbullying. The other factors that predicted being a perpetrator of cyberbullying were being a perpetrator of bullying, normative beliefs about aggression, moral disengagement, risky online behaviour, narcissism, frequency of Internet use, anger, reduced empathy, negative school climate, and high levels of parental monitoring.

Many young people who engage in cyberbullying have previously been involved in other forms of bullying, particularly face-to-face bullying (Raskauskas & Stoltz, 2007). For example, for university students from Hong Kong, experiencing cyberbullying is predictive of engaging in cyberbullying behaviours (Xiao & Wong, 2013). Although the co-occurrence between young people's involvement in cyberbullying and face-to-face bullying is complex, an emerging line of enquiry suggests that there is an element of causal progression from face-to-face bullying to cyberbullying. Specifically, those young people who have experienced face-to-face bullying often become perpetrators of cyberbullying (e.g., Connell et al., 2014; König, Gollwitzer, & Steffgen, 2010). Of those young people who were the target of face-to-face bullying, 41 % subsequently became 'avengers' (König et al., 2010). 'Avengers' direct their cyberbullying behaviours towards individuals who have previously bullied them in face-to-face settings. For a further discussion of the co-occurrence of face-to-face bullying and cyberbullying, see Chap. 5 Sect. 5.4.

In conclusion, this chapter has presented an overview of the current reported prevalence rates for the various roles in cyberbullying drawn from the existing literature (in Table 4.1). There is wide variation in these prevalence rates, and whilst these may reflect an actual variation, it is important to recognise that a number of methodological explanations may underpin this discrepancy. For example, the methods used to assess cyberbullying either at a global or specific level, the timeframe examined, and the conceptualisations of cyberbullying used by previous researchers have varied. There are also reported variations in prevalence rates of cyberbullying according to characteristics of the sample examined such as their age, sex, amount of time spent online, and the country of origin. Whilst there is no easy answer as to why this variation in the prevalence rates of cyberbullying occurs, it is important to be mindful of these factors when interpreting prevalence rates. Further, as Smith (2014) argues for face-to-face bullying, researchers examining cyberbullying must adopt a common definition so that prevalence rates can be robustly identified and examined. Adopting common definitions and methods will also allow us to make comparisons between samples, evaluate the effectiveness of anti-cyberbullying interventions, and understand the extent to which cyberbullying represents growing a problem. Finally, this chapter has reviewed some of the factors that predict involvement in cyberbullying either as a target or a perpetrator.

REFERENCES

Accordino, D. B., & Accordino, M. P. (2011). An exploratory study of face-to-face and cyberbullying in sixth grade students. *American Secondary Education, 40*, 14–30.

Ackers, M. J. (2012). Cyberbullying: Through the eyes of children and young people. *Educational Psychology in Practice: Theory, Research and Practice in Educational Psychology, 28*, 141–157.

Akbulut, Y., & Eristi, B. (2011). Cyberbullying and victimisation among Turkish university students. *Australasian Journal of Educational Technology, 27*, 1155–1170.

Allen, K. P. (2012). Off the radar and ubiquitous: Text messaging and its relationship to 'drama' and cyberbullying in an affluent, academically rigorous US high school. *Journal of Youth Studies, 15*, 99–117.

Álvarez-García, D., Núñez Pérez, J. C., Dobarro González, A., & Rodríguez Pérez, C. (2015). Risk factors associated with cybervictimization in adolescence. *International Journal of Clinical Health Psychology, 15*, 226–235.

Analitis, F., Velderman, M. K., Ravens-Sieberer, U., Detmar, S., Erhart, M., Berra, S., ... European Kidscreen Group. (2009). Being bullied: Associated factors in children and adolescents 8 to 18 years old in 11 European countries. *Pediatrics, 123*, 569–577.

Aricak, O. T. (2009). Psychiatric symptomatology as a predictor of cyberbullying among university students. *Eurasian Journal of Educational Research, 34*, 167–184.

Aricak, T., Siyahhan, S., Uzunhasanoglu, A., Saribeyoglu, S., Ciplak, S., Yilmaz, N., & Memmedov, C. (2008). Cyberbullying among Turkish adolescents. *CyberPsychology & Behavior, 11*, 253–261.

Bannink, R., Broeren, S., Van de Looij-Jansen, P. M., de Waart, F. G., & Raat, H. (2014). Cyber and traditional bullying victimization as a risk factor for mental health problems and suicidal ideation in adolescents. *PLOS ONE, 9*, e94026.

Barlett, C. P., Gentile, D. A., & Chew, C. (2014). Predicting cyberbullying from anonymity. *Psychology of Popular Media Culture*. Advanced online publication.

Bauman, S. (2010). Cyberbullying in a rural intermediate school: An exploratory study. *Journal of Early Adolescence, 30*, 803–833.

Bauman, S., & Newman, M. L. (2013). Testing assumptions about cyberbullying: Perceived distress associated with acts of conventional and cyber bullying. *Psychology of Violence, 3*, 27–38.

Beran, T., & Li, Q. (2005). Cyber-harassment: A study of a new method for an old behavior. *Journal of Educational Computing Research, 32*, 265–277.

Berne, S., Frisén, A., Schultze-Krumbholz, A., Scheithauer, H., Naruskov, K., Luik, P., ... Zukauskiene, R. (2013). Cyberbullying assessment instruments: A systematic review. *Aggression and Violent Behavior, 18*, 320–334.

Blakeney, K. (2012). An instrument to measure traditional and cyber bullying in overseas schools. *International Schools Journal, 32*, 45–54.

Brack, K., & Caltabiano, N. (2014). Cyberbullying and self-esteem in Australian adults. *Journal of Psychosocial Research on Cyberspace, 8*, article 7.

Brewer, G., & Kerslake, J. (2015). Cyberbullying, self-esteem, empathy and loneliness. *Computers in Human Behavior, 48*, 255–260.

Butler, D., Kift, S., & Campbell, M. (2009). Cyber bullying in schools and the law: Is there an effective means of addressing the power imbalance? *eLaw Journal: Murdoch University Electronic Journal of Law, 16*, 84–114.

Calvete, E., Orue, I., Estévez, A., Villardón, L., & Padilla, P. (2010). Cyberbullying in adolescents: Modalities and aggressors' profile. *Computers in Human Behavior, 26*, 1128–1135.

Connell, N. M., Schell-Bussey, N. M., Pearce, A. N., & Negro, P. (2014). Badgrlz? Exploring sex differences in cyberbullying behaviours. *Youth Violence and Juvenile Justice, 12*, 209–228.

Crosslin, K., & Crosslin, M. (2014). Cyberbullying at a Texas University—A mixed methods approach to examining online aggression. *Texas Public Health Journal, 66*, 26–31.

D'Anotona, R., Kevorkian, M., & Russom, A. (2010). Sexting, texting, cyberbullying and keeping youth safe online. *Journal of Social Sciences, 6*, 521–526.

Dehue, F. (2013). Cyberbullying research: New perspectives and alternative methodologies. Introduction to the special issue. *Journal of Community & Applied Social Psychology, 23*, 1–6.

Dehue, F., Bolman, C., & Völlink, T. (2008). Cyberbullying: Youngsters' experiences and parental perception. *CyberPsychology & Behavior, 11*, 217–223.

del Barco, B. L., Castaño, E. F., Bullón, F. F., & Carroza, T. G. (2012). Cyberbullying in a sample of secondary students: Modulating variables and social networks. *Electronic Journal of Research in Educational Psychology, 10*, 771–788.

Dempsey, A. G., Sulkowski, M. L., Nichols, R., & Storch, E. A. (2009). Differences between peer victimization in cyber and physical settings and associated psychosocial adjustment in early adolescence. *Psychology in the Schools, 46*, 962–972.

Didden, R., Scholte, R. H. J., Korzilius, H., De Moor, J. M. H., Vermeulen, A., O'Reilly, M., ... Lancioni, G. E. (2009). Cyberbullying among students with intellectual and developmental disability in special education settings. *Developmental Neurorehabilitation, 12*, 146–151.

Erdur-Baker, Ö. (2010). Cyberbullying and its correlation to traditional bullying, gender and frequent and risky usage on internet-mediated communication tools. *New Media & Society, 12*, 109–125.

Fanti, K. A., Demetriou, A. G., & Hawa, V. V. (2012). A longitudinal study of cyberbullying examining risk and protective factors. *European Journal of Developmental Psychology, 9*, 168–181.

Fenaughty, J., & Harré, N. (2013). Factors associated with distressing electronic harassment and cyberbullying. *Computers in Human Behavior, 29*, 803–811.

Festl, R., & Quandt, T. (2013). Social relations and cyberbullying: The influence of individual and structural attributes on victimization and perpetration via the internet. *Human Communication Research, 39*, 101–126.

Fletcher, A., Fitzgerald-Yau, N., Jones, R., Allen, E., Viner, R. M., & Bonell, C. (2014). Brief report: Cyberbullying perpetration and its associations with socio-demographics, aggressive behaviour at school, and mental health outcomes. *Journal of Adolescence, 37*, 1393–1398.

Gahagan, K., Vaterlus, J. M., & Frost, L. R. (2016). College student cyberbullying on social networking sites: Conceptualization, prevalence, and perceived bystander responsibility. *Computers in Human Behavior, 55*, 1097–1105.

Garaigordobil, M. (2015). Cyberbullying in adolescents and youth in the Basque country: Prevalence of cybervictims, cyberaggressors, and cyberobservers. *Journal of Youth Studies, 18*, 569–582.

Gofin, R., & Avitzour, M. (2012). Traditional versus internet bullying in junior high school students. *Maternal and Child Health Journal, 16*, 1625–1635.

Gomez-Garbiello, C., Shariff, S., McConnel, M., & Talwar, V. (2012). Adolescents' evaluation of cyberbullying events. *Alberta Journal of Educational Research, 58*, 474–477.

Görzig, A., & Frumkin, L. A. (2013). Cyberbullying experiences on-the-go: When social media can become distressing. *Cyberpsychology: Journal of Psychosocial Research on Cyberspace, 7*, article 4.

Gradinger, P., Strochmeier, D., & Spiel, C. (2009). Traditional bullying and cyberbullying: Identification of risk groups for adjustment problems. *Zeitschrift für Psychologie/Journal of Psychology, 217*, 205–213.

Gradinger, P., Strohmeier, D., & Spiel, C. (2010). Definition and measurement of cyberbullying. *Cyberpsychology: Journal of Psychosocial Research on Cyberspace, 4*, 1–13.

Hinduja, S., & Patchin, J. W. (2008). Personal information of adolescents on the Internet: A quantitative content analysis of MySpace. *Journal of Adolescence, 31*, 125–146.

Holfeld, B., & Leadbeater, B. J. (2015). The nature and frequency of cyber bullying behaviors and victimization experiences in young Canadian children. *Canadian Journal of School Psychology, 30*, 116–135.

Juvonen, J., & Gross, E. F. (2008). Extending the school grounds?—Bullying experiences in cyberspace. *Journal of School Health, 78*, 496–505.

Katzer, C., Fetchenhauer, D., & Belschak, F. (2009). Cyberbullying: Who are the victims? A comparison of victimization in internet chatrooms and victimization in school. *Journal of Media Psychology, 21*, 25–36.

Kite, S. L., Gable, R., & Filippelli, L. (2010). Assessing middle school students' knowledge of conduct and consequences and their behaviours regarding the use of social networking sites. *The Clearing House, 83*, 158–163.

Kokkinos, C. M., Balzidis, E., & Xynogala, D. (2016). Prevalence and personality correlates of Facebook bullying among university students. *Computers in Human Behavior, 55*, 840–850.

König, A., Gollwitzer, M., & Steffgen, G. (2010). Cyberbullying as an act of revenge? *Australian Journal of Guidance & Counselling, 20*, 210–224.

Kowalski, R. M., Giumetti, G. W., Schroeder, A. N., & Lattanner, M. R. (2014). Bulling in the digital age: A critical review and meta-analysis of cyberbullying research among youth. *Psychological Bulletin, 140*, 1073–1137.

Kowalski, R. M., & Limber, S. P. (2007). Electronic bullying among middle school students. *Journal of Adolescent Health, 41*, S22–S30.

Kubiszewksi, V., Fontaine, R., Potard, C., & Auzoult, L. (2015). Does cyberbullying overlap with school bullying when taking modality of involvement into account? *Computers in Human Behavior, 43*, 49–57.

Kwan, G. C. E., & Skoric, M. M. (2013). Facebook bullying: An extension of battles in school. *Computers in Human Behavior, 29*, 16–25.

Låftman, S. B., Modin, B., & Östberg, V. (2013). Cyberbullying and subjective health. A largescale study of students in Stockholm, Sweden. *Children and Youth Services Review, 35*, 112–119.

Lam, L. T., Cheng, Z., & Liu, X. (2013). Violent online games exposure and cyberbullying/victimization among adolescents. *Cyberpsychology, Behavior, and Social Networking, 16*, 159–164.

Lapidot-Lefler, N., & Dolev-Cohen, M. (2015). Comparing cyberbullying and school bullying among school students: Prevalence, gender, and grade level differences. *Social Psychology of Education, 18*, 1–6.

Lemstra, M., Rogers, M., Redgate, L., Garner, M., & Moraros, J. (2011). Prevalence, risk indicators and outcomes of bullying among On-Reserve First Nations youth. *Canadian Journal of Public Health, 102*, 462–466.

Li, Q. (2006). Cyberbullying in schools: A research of gender differences. *School Psychology International, 27*, 157–170.

Li, Q. (2007a). New bottle but old wine: A research of cyberbullying in schools. *Computers in Human Behavior, 23*, 1777–1791.

Li, Q. (2007b). Bullying in the new playground: Research into cyberbullying and cyber victimization. *Australasian Journal of Educational Technology, 23*, 435–454.

Li, Q. (2008). A cross-cultural comparison of adolescents' experience related to cyberbullying. *Educational Research, 50*, 223–234.

MacDonald, C. D., & Roberts-Pittman, B. (2010). Cyberbullying among college students: Prevalence and demographic differences. *Procedia Social and Behavioral Sciences, 9*, 2003–2009.

Mark, L., & Ratliffe, K. T. (2011). Cyber worlds: New playgrounds for bullying. *Computers in the Schools, 28,* 92–116.

Marsh, L., McGee, R., Nada-Raja, S., & Williams, S. (2010). Brief report: Text bullying and traditional bullying among New Zealand secondary school students. *Journal of Adolescence, 33,* 237–240.

Menesini, E., & Nocentini, A. (2009). Cyberbullying definition and measurement: Some critical considerations. *Zeitschrift für Psychologie/Journal of Psychology, 217,* 230–232.

Menesini, E., Nocentini, A., & Calussi, P. (2011). The measurement of cyberbullying: Dimensional structure and relative item severity and discrimination. *Cyberpsychology, Behavior, and Social Networking, 14,* 267–274.

Mesch, G. S. (2009). Parental mediation, online activities, and cyberbullying. *CyberPsychology & Behavior, 12,* 387–393.

Metwally, S., & Betts, L. R. (2015, May). "It won't happen to me"—The Third Person Effect and Cyberbullying. Poster presented at the *British Psychological Society Annual Conference,* Liverpool.

Mishna, F., Saini, M., & Solomon, S. (2009). Ongoing and online: Children and youth's perceptions of cyber bullying. *Children and Youth Services Review, 31,* 1222–1228.

Modecki, K. L., Barber, B. L., & Vernon, L. (2013). Mapping developmental precursors of cyber-aggression: Trajectories of risk predict perpetration and victimization. *Journal of Youth and Adolescence, 42,* 651–661.

Monks, C. P., Robinson, S., & Worlidge, P. (2012). The emergence of cyberbullying: A survey of primary school pupils' perceptions and experiences. *School Psychology International, 33,* 477–491.

Moore, P. M., Huebner, E. S., & Hills, K. J. (2012). Electronic bullying and cybervictimization and life satisfaction in middle school students. *Social Indicators Research, 107,* 429–447.

Morgan, H. (2012). What teachers and schools can do to control the growing problem of school bullying. *The Clearing House, 85,* 174–178.

Navarro, R., Yubero, S., Larrañaga, E., & Martínez, V. (2012). Children's cyberbullying victimization: Associations with social anxiety and social competence in a Spanish sample. *Child Indicators Research, 5,* 281–295.

Olenik-Shemesh, D., Heiman, T., & Eden, S. (2012). Cyberbullying victimisation in adolescence: Relationships with loneliness and depressive mood. *Emotional and Behavioural Difficulties, 17,* 361–374.

Olweus, D. (2012a). Cyberbullying: An overrated phenomenon? *European Journal of Developmental Psychology, 9,* 520–538.

Olweus, D. (2012b). Comments on cyberbullying: A rejoinder. *European Journal of Developmental Psychology, 9,* 559–568.

Olweus, D. (2013). School bullying: Development and some important challenges. *Annual Review of Clinical Psychology, 9,* 751–780.

Ortega, R., Calmaestra, J., & Mora-Merchán, J. (2008). Cyberbullying. *International Journal of Psychology and Psychological Therapy, 8,* 183–192.

Ortega, R., Elipe, P., Moran-Merchán, J. A., Genta, M. L., Brighi, A., Guraini, A., … Tippett, A. (2009). The emotional impact of bullying and cyberbullying on victims: A European cross-national study. *Aggressive Behavior, 38,* 342–356.

Pabian, S., & Vandebosch, H. (2014). Using the theory of planned behaviour to understand cyberbullying: The importance of beliefs for developing interventions. *European Journal of Developmental Psychology, 11,* 463–477.

Patchin, J. W., & Hinduja, S. (2006). Bullies move beyond the schoolyard: A preliminary look at cyberbullying. *Youth Violence and Juvenile Justice, 4,* 148–169.

Paullet, K., & Pinchot, J. (2014). Behind the screen where today's bully plays: Perceptions of college students on cyberbullying. *Journal of Information Systems Education, 25,* 63–69.

Pedersen, S. (2013). UK young adults' safety awareness online—Is it a 'girl' thing? *Journal of Youth Studies, 16,* 404–419.

Pelfrey, W. V., Jr., & Weber, N. L. (2013). Keyboard gangsters: Analysis of incidence and correlates of cyberbullying in a large urban student population. *Deviant Behavior, 34,* 68–84.

Popović-Ćitić, B., Djurić, S., & Cvetković, V. (2011). The prevalence of cyberbullying among adolescents: A case study of middle schools in Serbia. *School Psychology International, 32,* 412–424.

Price, M., Chin, M. A., Higa-McMillan, C., Kim, S., & Frueh, B. C. (2013). Prevalence and internalizing problems of ethnoracially diverse victims of traditional and cyber bullying. *School Mental Health, 5,* 183–191.

Pyzalski, J. (2012). From cyberbullying to electronic aggression: Typology of the phenomenon. *Emotional and Behavioural Difficulties, 17,* 305–317.

Raskauskas, J., & Stoltz, A. D. (2007). Involvement in traditional and electronic bullying among adolescents. *Developmental Psychology, 43,* 564–575.

Reeckman, B., & Cannard, L. (2009). Cyberbullying: A TAFE perspective. *Youth Studies Australia, 28,* 41–49.

Sakellariou, T., Carroll, A., & Houghton, S. (2012). Rates of cyber cybervictimization and bullying among male Australian primary and high school students. *School Psychology International, 33,* 533–549.

Schenk, A. M., & Fremouw, W. J. (2012). Prevalence, psychological impact, and coping of cyberbully cybervictims among college students. *Journal of School Violence, 11,* 21–37.

Schneider, S. K., O'Donnell, L., Stueve, A., & Coulter, R. W. S. (2012). Cyberbullying, school bullying, and psychological distress: A regional census of high school students. *American Journal of Public Health, 102,* 171–177.

Schultze-Krumbholz, A., & Scheithauer, H. (2009). Social-behavioral correlates of cyberbullying in a German student sample. *Zeitschrift für Psychologie/Journal of Psychology, 217,* 224–226.

Schultze-Krumbholz, A., Göbel, K., Scheithauer, H., Brighi, A., Guarini, A., ... Smith, P. K. (2015). A comparison of classification approaches for cyberbulling and traditional bullying using data from six European countries. *Journal of School Violence, 14,* 47–65.

Selkie, E. M., Kota, R., Chan, Y.-F., & Moreno, M. (2015). Cyberbullying, depression, and problem alcohol use in female college students: A multisite study. *Cyberpsychology, Behavior, and Social Networking, 18,* 79–86.

Sengupta, A., & Chaudhuri, A. (2011). Are social networking sites a source of online harassment for teens? Evidence from survey data. *Children and Youth Service Review, 33,* 284–290.

Ševčíková, A., & Šmahel, D. (2009). Online harassment and cyberbullying in the Czech Republic: Comparison across age groups. *Zeitschrift für Psychologie/ Journal of Psychology, 217,* 227–229.

Slonje, R., Smith, P. K., & Frisén, A. (2013). The nature of cyberbullying, and strategies for prevention. *Computers in Human Behavior, 29,* 26–32.

Smith, P. K. (2014). *Understanding school bullying: Its nature & prevention strategies.* London: Sage.

Smith, P., Mahdavi, J., Carvalho, M., Fisher, S., Russell, S., & Tippett, N. (2008). Cyberbullying: Its nature and impact in secondary school pupils. *The Journal of Child Psychology and Psychiatry, 49,* 376–385.

Spenser, K. A., & Betts, L. R. (2014, May). "People think it's a harmless joke when really it could be hurting someone": Young people's experiences of cyber bullying. Poster presented at the *British Psychological Society Annual Conference,* International Convention Centre, Birmingham.

Thomas, S. P. (2006). From the editor—The phenomenon of cyberbullying. *Issues in Mental Health Nursing, 27,* 1015–1016.

Turan, N., Polat, O., Karapirli, M., Uysal, C., & Turan, S. G. (2011). The new violence type of the era: Cyber bullying among university students. *Neurology, Psychiatry and Brian Research, 17,* 21–26.

Vandebosch, H., & van Cleemput, K. (2009). Cyberbullying among youngsters: Profiles of bullies and victims. *New Media & Society, 11,* 1349–1371.

Vieno, A., Gini, G., & Santinello, M. (2011). Different forms of bullying and their association to smoking and drinking behavior in Italian adolescents. *Journal of School Health, 81,* 393–399.

Wachs, S. (2012). Moral disengagement and emotional and social difficulties in bullying and cyberbullying: Differences by participant role. *Emotional and Behavioural Difficulties, 17,* 347–360.

Wade, A., & Beran, T. (2011). Cyberbullying: The new era of bullying. *Canadian Journal of School Psychology, 26,* 44–61.

Walrave, M., & Heirman, W. (2011). Cyberbullying: Predicting cybervictimization and cyberaggression. *Children & Society, 25,* 59–72.

Wang, J., Iannotti, R. J., & Luk, J. W. (2012). Patterns of adolescent bullying behaviours: Physical, verbal, exclusion, rumor, and cyber. *Journal of School Psychology, 50*, 521–534.

Wang, J., Iannotti, R. J., & Nansel, T. R. (2009). School bullying among adolescents in the United States: Physical, verbal, relational, and cyber. *Journal of Adolescent Health, 45*, 368–375.

Wegge, D., Vandebosch, H., & Eggermont, S. (2014). Who bullies whom online: A social network analysis of cyberbullying in a school context. *Communications, 39*, 415–433.

Wensley, K., & Campbell, M. (2012). Heterosexual and nonhetrosexual young university students' involvement in traditional and cyber forms of bullying. *Cyberpsychology, Behavior, and Social Networking, 15*, 649–654.

West, D. (2015). An investigation into the prevalence of cyberbullying among students aged 16–19 in post-compulsory education. *Research in Post-Compulsory Education, 20*, 96–112.

Whittaker, E., & Kowalski, R. M. (2015). Cyberbullying via social media. *Journal of School Violence, 14*, 11–29.

Williams, K. R., & Guerra, N. G. (2007). Prevalence and predictors of internet bullying. *Journal of Adolescent Health, 41*, S14–S21.

Wolak, J., Mitchell, K. J., & Finkelhor, D. (2007). Does online harassment constitute bullying? An exploration of online harassment by known peers and online-only contacts. *Journal of Adolescent Health, 41*, S51–S58.

Wright, M. F., & Li, Y. (2013). Normative beliefs about aggression and cyber aggression among young adults: A longitudinal investigation. *Aggressive Behavior, 39*, 161–170.

Wright, V. H., Burnham, J. J., Inman, C. T., & Ogorchock, H. N. (2009). Cyberbullying: Using virtual scenarios to educate and raise awareness. *Journal of Computing in Teacher Education, 26*, 35–41.

Xiao, B. S., & Wong, Y. M. (2013). Cyber-bullying among university students: An empirical investigation from the social cognitive perspective. *International Journal of Business and Information, 8*, 34–69.

Ybarra, M. L. (2003). Linkages between depressive symptomatology and internet harassment among young regular internet users. *CyberPsychology & Behavior, 7*, 247–257.

Ybarra, M. L., Diener-West, M., & Leaf, P. J. (2007). Examining the overlap in internet harassment and school bullying: Implications for school intervention. *Journal of Adolescent Health, 41*, S42–S50.

Ybarra, M. L., & Mitchell, K. J. (2004). Online aggressors/targets, aggressors, and targets: A comparison of associated youth characteristics. *Journal of Child Psychology and Psychiatry, 45*, 1308–1316.

Yilmaz, H. (2011). Cyberbullying in Turkish middle schools: An exploratory study. *School Psychology International, 32*, 645–654.

CHAPTER 5

The Consequences of Cyberbullying

Abstract Given the pervasiveness of cyberbullying in everyday life, researchers have begun to explore the consequences of involvement in cyberbullying for both the perpetrator and the target. There is emerging evidence that involvement in cyberbullying is associated with psychosocial adjustment, general adjustment, suicide, and subsequent involvement in cyberbullying. Although, to date, many of the studies have been cross-sectional nature, meaning that causality cannot be established, some longitudinal studies have started to document the longer-term consequences of involvement in cyberbullying. This chapter will provide a summary of the research that has examined the consequences of involvement in cyberbullying for young people.

Keywords Cyberbullying • Psychosocial adjustment • Mental well-being • Suicide • Adjustment • Academic performance • Health

This chapter will discuss the emerging research that has explored the consequences of experiencing and engaging in cyberbullying. Consequently, the chapter will consider the effects of involvement in cyberbullying from the perspective of both the target and the perpetrator. Traditionally, it had been suggested that the targets of face-to-face bullying are more likely to experience adverse consequences as a result of their experiences, although more recently, the consequences for all parties involved in bullying tend

© The Editor(s) (if applicable) and The Author(s) 2016
L.R. Betts, *Cyberbullying*, DOI 10.1057/978-1-137-50009-0_5

to be examined. Therefore, the consequences of face-to-face bullying are widely recognised for both the perpetrator and the target; however, debate has occurred as to whether similar consequences exist for cyberbullying. For example, some researchers argue that the consequences of cyberbullying are less extreme than those associated with face-to-face bullying (e.g., Bauman & Newman, 2013). The relative 'newness' of cyberbullying, compared to face-to-face bullying, and the evolving nature of digital technology, means that our understanding of the consequences of being involved in cyberbullying is in their infancy. However, there is growing empirical evidence that there are consequences associated with experiencing cyberbullying either as a perpetrator or a target.

Notwithstanding the relative 'newness' of cyberbullying, 93 % of young people who experience cyberbullying as a target, report that their experiences have affected them (Raskauskas & Stoltz, 2007). The most common way identified by young people was experiencing emotional reactions such as feeling sad, helpless, or depressed. Moreover, following a review of existing research findings, Nixon (2014) argued that cyberbullying represents an 'emerging international public health concern, related to serious mental health concerns, with significant impact on adolescents' depression, anxiety, self-esteem, emotional distress, substance use, and suicidal behaviour' (p. 154). Therefore, this chapter will begin by considering the consequences of involvement in cyberbullying with regard to psychosocial adjustment and general adjustment. Next, the chapter will present evidence that involvement in cyberbullying and face-to-face bullying is a specific outcome of experiencing in cyberbullying. Subsequently, in line with some of the themes that have been touched upon previously in this book, the chapter will consider the association between cyberbullying and suicide. The chapter will then discuss the extent to which the consequences of cyberbullying are dependent on the perpetrator, media, and audience. Finally, having reviewed the literature, the chapter will return to the question about whether there are, indeed, consequences associated with involvement in cyberbullying.

5.1   Psychosocial Adjustment Consequences

The term "psychosocial adjustment" encompasses a range of variables that impact on an individual's well-being and social relationships. Broadly speaking, researchers have tended to examine the association between cyberbullying and young people's mental well-being, self-esteem, and social relationships. The evidence for each of these associations will be discussed in turn.

Mental well-being. A number of studies have reported that experiences of cyberbullying are associated with young people's mental well-being. For example, young people from Japan who reported that they were the target of cyberbullying were also more likely to report having poorer mental health than those who were not targets (Imamura et al., 2009). Similarly, being the target of cyberbullying is also associated with higher levels of psychological distress compared to those not involved in cyberbullying, although the reported levels of distress associated with cyberbullying were lower than if the young person was the target of face-to-face bullying (Kubiszewksi, Fontaine, Potard, & Auzoult, 2015). Whilst concurrent associations between cyberbullying and general mental well-being have been reported, recent longitudinal research conducted over two years by Bannink, Broeren, Van de Looij-Jansen, de Waart, and Raat (2014) suggests that the pattern of association between cyberbullying and general mental well-being may be more complex. Cyberbullying was not associated with mental ill health in boys when their baseline mental health was controlled for. However, in girls, cyberbullying was associated with mental ill health after controlling for mental health at baseline. Together, Bannink et al.'s findings suggest that gender may moderate the relationship between cyberbullying and mental well-being. There is also evidence to suggest that it is not just the targets of cyberbullying who experience mental well-being difficulties. For example, some perpetrators of cyberbullying also suffer from mental ill health compared to those who do not engage in such behaviours (Campbell, Slee, Spears, Butler, & Kift, 2013).

One frequently examined facet of mental well-being is depression and depressive symptoms (the term used when a clinical diagnosis of depression is not made). Young people who experience cyberbullying also report elevated levels of depressive symptoms compared to those not involved in cyberbullying, and this relationship holds when involvement in face-to-face bullying is controlled for (Perren, Dooley, Shaw, & Cross, 2010). Similarly, engaging in higher levels of cyberbullying behaviours as a perpetrator is also associated with elevated depressive symptoms (Campbell et al., 2013; McDermott, 2012). Involvement in cyberbullying has also been found to increase the odds of experiencing depression across all cyberbullying roles (Selkie, Kota, Chan, & Moreno, 2015). Young people who fulfilled the target, perpetrator, or perpetrator/target roles were more likely to experience depression than those young people who did not fulfil these roles.

The cyberbullying behaviours that increased the odds of experiencing depression the most were experiencing unwanted sexual advances online or via text messages. In other words, if young people experienced unwanted sexual advances, then they were more likely to develop depression. Similar findings have also been reported in young people who have intellectual and developmental disabilities: Being the target of cyberbullying via the Internet or mobile telephone was associated with higher levels of depression (Didden et al., 2009).

In addition to the concurrent associations between cyberbullying involvement and depressive symptoms, which have been reported when cyberbullying involvement and depressive symptoms are assessed at a single time-point, longitudinal studies have also reported similar findings. For example, young people who experience cyberbullying are likely to experience elevated depressive symptoms over time (Landoll, La Greca, Lai, Chan, & Herge, 2015; Machmutow, Perren, Sticca & Alsaker, 2012). Further, this finding is exacerbated for those classified as 'stable victims': Young people who remain targets of cyberbullying are likely to report elevated levels of depressive symptoms over time (Gámez-Guadix, Gini, & Calvete, 2015). Together, these studies suggest that there is some association between involvement in cyberbullying, irrespective of a role that an individual fulfils, and depressive symptoms, and this finding has been replicated in a number of samples drawn from different populations. However, not all studies that have examined the association between cyberbullying involvement and depression have reported significant associations between these variables (e.g., Dempsey, Sulkowski, Nichols, & Storch, 2009; Goebert, Else, Matsu, Chung-Do, & Chang, 2011). Therefore, these studies suggest that whilst depression and depressive symptoms may increase with involvement in cyberbullying, it is not always inevitable.

Another facet of mental well-being that has been examined by researchers with regard to cyberbullying is anxiety. Experiencing cyberbullying is associated with various forms of anxiety. For example, those young people who are the target of cyberbullying report experiencing greater levels of general anxiety (Juvonen & Gross, 2008; Price, Chin, Higa-McMillan, Kim, & Frueh, 2013). A similar relationship has also been identified between experiencing cyberbullying as a target and elevated levels of social anxiety (Dempsey et al., 2009; Landoll et al., 2015). Specifically, those young people who experience higher levels of cyberbullying are more likely to report experiencing higher levels of anxiety in social situations. Lam, Cheng, and Liu (2013) also reported that the association between involvement in cyberbullying and anxiety occurred for both perpetrators and targets of cyberbullying such that perpetrators and targets of cyberbullying were more likely to experience anxiety. However, as with research on cyberbullying and depressive symptoms, some studies have failed to replicate the relationship between experiencing cyberbullying and anxiety (e.g., Goebert et al., 2011).

Self-esteem. The relationship between face-to-face bullying and self-esteem has been clearly established in the previous research (e.g., Hawker & Boulton, 2000). The research consistently reports that those young people who experience face-to-face bullying report experiencing lower self-esteem. Similar associations have also been reported for cyberbullying and self-esteem: Patchin and Hinduja (2010) identified that both perpetrators and targets of cyberbullying reported that they had lower levels of self-esteem compared to those young people who were not involved in cyberbullying. Moreover, the relationship between experiencing cyberbullying and self-esteem is also unique and distinct from the impact of other forms of bullying (Cénat et al., 2014). Specifically, experiencing cyberbullying is predictive of lower self-esteem, and this relationship occurs when other experiences of bullying are controlled for. These patterns of association between cyberbullying involvement and self-esteem have also been reported in non-typically developing samples. For example, Didden et al. (2009) reported that young people with intellectual and developmental disabilities who were the target of cyberbullying, either via the Internet or mobile telephones, reported having lower self-esteem. Further, those young people who engaged in cyberbullying via a mobile telephone also reported that they had lower self-esteem. In addition to self-esteem being directly associated with, and impacted on by, involvement in cyberbullying, a target's self-esteem can also act as protective factor from the effects of cyberbullying. Specifically, higher levels of self-esteem can serve to 'buffer' or protect a target from some of the negative consequences associated with experiencing cyberbullying (Álvarez-García, Núñez Pérez, Dobarro González, & Rodríguez Pérez, 2015).

Social relationships. Involvement in cyberbullying can also impact on many aspects of young people's social relationships. At a general level, irrespective of the role young people fulfil within a cyberbullying episode, those that are involved in cyberbullying are perceived to be less popular by their peers (Festl & Quandt, 2013). At a more specific level, involvement in cyberbullying can result in changes in social relationship formation and maintenance, and changes in an individual's social reputation and desirability as an interaction partner. Both of these aspects will be discussed in turn.

Focusing on how involvement in cyberbullying can change aspects of social relationship formation and maintenance, young people who are targets of cyberbullying may become reticent in social situations and withdraw from interactions with others. Therefore, because of their experiences of cyberbullying, targets of cyberbullying may seek to avoid social contact with peers. For example, in a sample of American University students, Crosslin and Crosslin (2014) found that those who had experienced cyberbullying were weary of interacting with new friends. Further, because of their experiences of cyberbullying participants also reported that they were less trusting of others, especially new interaction partners. Similarly, Rivituso (2014) reported that college students who repeatedly were the target of cyberbullying described how they felt vulnerable and their experiences fostered a general sense of mistrust in others. The undermining of an individual's trusting orientation should not be underestimated: Trust is an important factor in social relationship formation and maintenance (Rotenberg, 1994). The propensity to generally trust others not only facilitates relationship development but also results in more positive and satisfying social relationships.

Aligned to undermining the young people's trust in their social interaction partners, experiencing cyberbullying also impacts on how young people perceive and behave with their interaction partners. For example, 42.5% of targets of cyberbullying report that they feel frustrated with others and 40% report feeling angry (Patchin & Hinduja, 2006), and these feelings may, in turn, hinder their social relationships. More recently, evidence suggests that the impact of experiencing cyberbullying extends beyond perceived emotions when interacting with others to beliefs about the nature of these interactions (Jackson & Cohen, 2012). Jackson and Cohen reported that, for 3rd to 6th graders, experiencing cyberbullying as a target was associated with less optimism about peer relationships, fewer reported friendships, and lower social acceptance.

Young people's involvement in cyberbullying has also been associated with their social reputation and desirability as an interaction partner. Whilst targets of cyberbullying tend to be less popular amongst peers (Katzer, Fetchenhauer, & Belschak, 2009), perpetrators of cyberbullying often tend to be well integrated into the social sphere and regarded as desirable interaction partners by their peers. One group of perpetrators who are perceived as particularly desirable interaction partners are socially integrated bullies. Rodkin and Fischer (2012) argue that socially integrated bullies, who have higher social status than other perpetrators, engage in cyberbullying behaviours because they want to avoid becoming a target of other perpetrators. The strategy implemented by these socially integrated bullies is regarded as adaptive and functional because it is a protection mechanism. The protection comes from acting as a perpetrator which means that their reputation will spread and protect them from becoming a target of cyberbullying. However, not all perpetrators of cyberbullying have such high levels of social integration, some young people who engage in cyberbullying also report that they experience social difficulties (Campbell et al., 2013) and lower levels of peer support (Calvete, Orue, Estévez, Villardón, & Padilla, 2010).

Together, these studies provide growing evidence that involvement in cyberbullying, both from the perspective of the target and perpetrator is associated with a range of psychosocial outcomes. However, it is important to remember that many of these studies are correlational in nature and that further research is needed to examine the longitudinal impact of involvement in cyberbullying. The next section of this chapter will consider the more general impacts of cyberbullying involvement, including reputational, academic, and health related.

5.2   General Consequences

Owing to the unique nature of cyberbullying, alongside the psychosocial adjustment consequences of cyberbullying outlined in the previous section of this chapter, the impact of cyberbullying can extend further into an individual's life. Specifically, despite legislation within Europe and campaigns concerning 'the right to forget' (Rosen, 2012), the permanence of material posted in cyberspace means that an individual's actions may remain with them for years to come because of the lasting 'digital footprint'. The digital footprint means that people's interactions in the digital world can be subsequently reviewed by users for years to come (as exemplified by the case of Ghyslain Raza discussed in Chap. 3 Sect. 3.2). Consequently, whereas in face-to-face bullying, actions and behaviours are likely to be forgotten relatively quickly, with cyberbullying actions and behaviours may be taken out of context or retained over a lifetime. Therefore, as Borgia and Myers (2010) argue, one of the consequences associated with cyberbullying is the potential damage to an individual's reputation and their reputation loss as they move through adulthood.

My own recent research has revealed that young people are aware of the potential consequences of their actions during their teenage years (Spenser

& Betts, 2014). In a series of focus groups, young people talked about how their current behaviour could follow them into adulthood and impact adversely on their educational and career prospects. The young people were aware that potential future employers are likely to look at their social media profiles during the recruitment process. Although some argue that employers should refrain from viewing candidates' social network profiles (e.g., Clark & Roberts, 2010), it seems that the perceptions of the young people are correct as there is increasing evidence that potential employers carry out such checks (e.g., Berkelaar & Buzzanell, 2014). Indeed, it has been suggested that the 'digital footprint' likely acts as a mechanism through which reputational bias can operate (O'Keefe, Clarke-Pearson, & Council on Communication and Media, 2011).

In addition to impacting on an individual's reputation, involvement in cyberbullying also impacts on young people's experiences of education. Whilst cyberbullying predominately occurs outside of the school environment, one of the biggest reported impacts of cyberbullying involvement is on young people's engagement with school and their academic attainment: Up to one-third of young people report that their experiences of cyberbullying affect them at school (Patchin & Hinduja, 2006). For some young people, experiencing cyberbullying makes them afraid to go to school (Raskauskas & Stoltz, 2007), and this fear is further exacerbated when cyberbullying is combined with face-to-face bullying (Cross, Lester, & Barnes, 2015). The fear of attending school can also escalate to school avoidance such that young people may not attend school as a result of their cyberbullying experiences (West, 2015). Young people also report that experiencing cyberbullying makes them feel less safe at school (Sourander et al., 2010). In support of this finding, Bayar and Ucanok (2012) reported that young people not involved in cyberbullying perceived school and teachers more positively than perpetrators and perpetrator/targets of cyberbullying. Targets of cyberbullying also perceive their teachers more positively than perpetrators of cyberbullying, and those not involved in cyberbullying perceive other students more positively.

Similar associations to those for cyberbullying and school engagement have also been reported for experiencing Internet harassment (Ybarra, Diener-West, & Leaf, 2007): Being the target of Internet harassment was associated with two or more detentions or suspensions at school and skipping school over the last year. Also, those young people who experienced Internet harassment were 8 times more likely to report taking a weapon in to school in the last 30 days. Additionally, the impact of cyber harassment on academic achievement and adjustment extends beyond compulsory schooling. For example, 18% of university students who report that they were the targets of cyber harassment also reported that they experienced poor concentration, 10% low achievement, and 7.7% absenteeism (Beran, Rinaldi, Bickham, & Rich, 2012).

Considering how young people perceive school, and those they interact with at school, is important because there is evidence that perceptions of school and school relationships are associated with academic performance. Specifically, those young people who have more favourable attitudes towards school and higher aspirations perform better academically (Abu-Hilal, 2000). However, it is important to note that not all research studies have reported a negative association between cyberbullying involvement and academic performance. For example, Li (2007) reported that half of the targets of cyberbullying in their sample had above average school grades. However, because Li's study was cross-sectional in nature, it is possible that some of the young people were targeted because of their academic performance.

In addition to the evidence that experiencing cyberbullying as a target impacts on involvement in school and academic performance, similar evidence is also emerging for perpetrators. For example, involvement in cyberbullying as a perpetrator has been associated with more negative attitudes towards school (Pyzalski, 2012): Young people who are perpetrators of cyberbullying feel more negative about school. The majority of the research conducted to date that has examined the relationship between cyberbullying and academic performance has done so using correlational designs with young people. However, a study by Giumetti et al. (2013) experimentally manipulated workplace incivility over email akin to a form of cyberbullying. The results indicated that when uncivil email communications were received, this reduced performance on a maths task compared to when supportive communications were received suggesting that the content of electronic communication impacted on their performance.

As well as impacting on young people's academic performance, involvement in cyberbullying is also associated with other negative outcomes for young people's general adjustment. For example, Spears, Slee, Owens, and Johnson (2009) found that young people who experience cyberbullying were more likely to report that it caused disruption to their day-to-day activities compared to those young people not involved in cyberbullying. Similarly, experiencing cyberbullying has also been found to impact on young people's health with associations reported between being the target of cyberbullying and elevated somatic symptoms (Gradinger, Strochmeier, & Spiel, 2009). Further, being involved with cyberbullying either as a target or a perpetrator has been associated with skipping breakfast which is a health concern (Sampasa-Kanyinga, Roumeliotis, Farrow, & Shi, 2014). Other examples of how experiencing cyberbullying impacts on young people's health behaviour include binge drinking and marijuana use. Experiencing cyberbullying makes young people 2.5 times more likely to engage in binge drinking and marijuana use (Goebert et al., 2011). There is also longitudinal evidence that young people who continue to be targets of cyberbullying are more likely to report problematic alcohol use compared to other groups (Gámez-Guadix et al., 2015).

In summary, the research evidence suggests that involvement in cyberbullying is associated with a range of more general outcomes, including impacts on an individual's reputation, academic performance, and health. The next section of this chapter will focus on a very specific consequence of cyberbullying: Suicide.

5.3   SUICIDE

There is growing concern that involvement in cyberbullying, particularly as a target, is an antecedent of suicide. The research has focused on reported suicide attempts and suicidal ideation. Young people who are targets of cyberbullying and bias-based harassment (relating to race, ethnicity, or sexual orientation) are 7.85 times more likely to have attempted suicide (Sinclair, Bauman, Poteat, Boeing, & Russell, 2012). Further, young people who were targets of cyberbullying without bias-based harassment were 3.82 times more likely to have attempted suicide. Focusing on suicidal ideation, researchers report that there is an association between experiencing cyberbullying and suicidal ideation (Hinduja & Patchin, 2010). In other words, experiencing cyberbullying is associated with greater and more frequent thoughts of suicide. More recently, DeSmet et al. (2014) reported a similar association between cyberbullying experiences and suicidal ideation in a specific sample: Obese adolescents who experienced higher levels of cyberbullying were more likely to report higher levels of suicidal ideation.

Of course, not all young people who experience cyberbullying go on to have suicidal thoughts or, indeed, commit suicide. Consequently, a number of studies have investigated the mediators in the relationship between cyberbullying involvement and suicidal behaviours; for example, examining the role of depression (e.g., Sampasa-Kanyinga, Roumeliotis, & Xu, 2014). Sampasa-Kanyina et al. found that young people who are targets of cyberbullying also report higher suicidal ideation, plans, and suicide attempts, compared to those young people who have not had such experiences. Further, these relationships were fully mediated by depression suggesting that being a target of cyberbullying is associated with elevated feelings of depression and these elevated feelings of depression are predictive of suicide ideation, plans, and attempts. Substance use and violent behaviour have also been found to mediate the relationship between experiencing cyberbullying and suicidal behaviour (Litwiller & Brausch, 2013). Specifically, experiencing cyberbullying was predictive of higher levels of substance use and violent behaviour, and, together, these predicted suicidal behaviours. Litwiller and Brausch argue that this partial mediation occurred because substance use and violent behaviour habituate young people to physical pain and psychological anxiety, and this habituation, in turn, increases the risk of suicidal behaviours.

Consistent with the relationship between cyberbullying and suicidal behaviour, involvement in cyberbullying has also been associated with intentional self-harm (Lam et al., 2013). However, this pattern of a significant association between cyberbullying and suicidal ideation has not been replicated in all studies (e.g., Bannink et al., 2014). Bannink et al. account for the lack of association between cyberbullying and suicidal ideation because the age of their sample (first year secondary school age students) meant that the young people had a relatively short time to experience cyberbullying and, as such, the consequences of their experiences may not have been fully realised.

In addition to the research evidence that has explored the relationship between suicidal thoughts and cyberbullying, there are a number of high profile cases of cyber bullycide that have been reported in the media in the USA and UK. Bullycide was a term coined by Marr and Field (2001) to describe the phenomenon when young people committed suicide following experiences of school bullying. However, cyber bullycide is a term that is being increasingly used to describe cases where young people have committed suicide following their experiences of cyberbullying. A recent paper adopted a case study approach to examine young people's experiences of cyber bullying as possible antecedents in their suicide (Pendergrass & Wright, 2014). Pendergrass and Wright gained information on the cases of Amanda Todd, Jessica Laney, Rahtaeh Parsons, and Rebecca Ann Sedwick, through a range of secondary sources, including Google searches, print magazines and newspapers, radio and television broadcasts, and documentaries. Whilst the cyberbullying took many forms across these cases, two of these young people experienced an intensification of cyberbullying after they had shared explicit material. Further, common to all of the cases, the young people had tried to tackle the cyberbullying by moving schools but they continued to be targeted and had failed suicide attempts in the past.

Together, the research evidence and the high-profile cases from the media reveal that for some young people, one of the consequences of experiencing cyberbullying is suicide. However, it is important to remember that a number of factors mediate this relationship as it is not the case that all young people who experience cyberbullying subsequently commit suicide.

5.4   INVOLVEMENT IN CYBERBULLYING

Involvement in cyberbullying has been associated with aggression. Perpetrators of cyberbullying also display higher levels of overt and relational aggression (Gradinger et al., 2009) and are more likely to engage in proactive violence and justify their use of violence (Calvete et al., 2010) compared to those who were not perpetrators of cyberbullying. Individuals who are perpetrators of cyberbullying also have higher state and trait levels of anger compared to others, and cyber targets and perpetrators have higher state anger scores than young people not involved in cyberbullying (Lonigro et al., 2015). In addition to the elevated levels of aggression and aggressive acts associated with involvement in cyberbullying, there is an emerging line of research that suggests that one of the consequences of cyberbullying is further involvement in cyberbullying.

Young people who have experienced cyberbullying as a target are likely to engage in similar forms of behaviour directed towards others (Accordino & Accordino, 2011; Barlett & Gentile, 2012; Cuadrado-Gordillo & Fernández-Antelo, 2014). Cuadrado-Gordillo and Fernández-Antelo identified four groups of young people involved with face-to-face bullying and cyberbullying: traditional aggressive-victims, aggressive cyber-victims, cyberaggressive-victims, and cyberaggressive-cybervictims. The cyberaggressive-victims tended to be those young people who had experienced social exclusion and subsequently excluded others from social networks, disseminated compromising or ridiculing material, or made threats directed towards others. Further, young people who had experienced dissemination of compromising visual or audiovisual material were likely to engage in aggression and threats. Therefore, one of the consequences of experiencing cyberbullying as a target is engaging in such forms of cyberbullying behaviour as a perpetrator.

A potential explanation for why young people who experience cyberbullying subsequently engage in such behaviour is because of retaliation. Technology may afford young people with a relatively quick and easy way to retaliate (Wright & Li, 2013) that is not constrained by geographical proximity (Kite, Gable, & Filippelli, 2010). Through retaliation, young people can target the person who has cyberbullied them and 'get their own back'. Young people may justify their cyberbullying actions as retaliation and a form of protection against subsequent cyberbullying (Frey, Pearson, & Cohen, 2015). Of course, young people may also enter a cycle of retaliation and counter-retaliation which then serves to further perpetuate their experiences of cyberbullying and the adverse consequences associated with cyberbullying.

Retaliation may also explain why targets of face-to-face bullying subsequently become perpetrators of cyberbullying. According to the general strain theory, when applied to bullying, face-to-face bullying is likely to result in the young person experiencing negative strain (in the form of emotions and negative experiences) which, in turn, are externalised as cyberbullying behaviours (Jang, Song, & Kim, 2014). The general strain theory is also supported by the empirical work of Katzer et al. (2009) who reported that targets of cyberbullying often engage in cyberbullying behaviours in chatrooms as a mechanism to 'fight back' and 'let off steam'. Therefore, retaliation provides a mechanism for young people to redress the negative feelings experienced as a target (Varjas, Talley, Meyers, Parris, & Cutts, 2010) and simultaneously demonstrate that they are not an easy target (König, Gollwitzer, & Steffgen, 2010).

5.5   Consequences of Cyberbullying According to the Perpetrator, Audience, and Media

In addition to the range of consequences associated with involvement in cyberbullying, there is evidence that the effects of cyberbullying may vary according to a number of important factors. First, who the perpetrator is has an impact on the perception of the severity of the cyberbullying. The actions of an anonymous and unknown perpetrator were regarded as less impactful than the same actions from a known individual (Reeckman & Cannard, 2009). However, there is also evidence that the effects of cyberbullying on young people's social relationships may be exacerbated if the perpetrator of cyberbullying remains anonymous. Young people who do not know who is targeting them are likely to be weary and suspicious of those around them (Raskauskas & Stoltz, 2007). Second, the outcomes associated with cyberbullying are also likely to be more severe when the audience is larger and the behaviour highly visible (Dooley, Pyżalski, & Cross, 2009). Third, there is evidence that the impact of cyberbullying on the target may also vary according to the media. For example, Ortega et al. (2009) reported that distinct emotional responses occurred according to whether young people were targets of mobile telephone or Internet cyberbullying. Experiencing cyberbullying via a mobile telephone was associated with the following emotions: lonely, defenceless, depressed, stressed, afraid, and embarrassed. Conversely, experiencing cyberbullying via the Internet was associated with lonely, defenceless, depressed, stressed, afraid, embarrassed, worried, and upset. Fourth, the impact of cyberbullying experiences is also exacerbated when individuals report that they have a lack of control over what is happening to them (Rivituso, 2014).

5.6   ARE THERE REALLY CONSEQUENCES OF CYBERBULLYING?

Despite the wide range of literature that has been reviewed so far in this chapter, it is important to question to what extent all young people who are involved in cyberbullying experience consequences. As with the general bullying literature, there is debate about whether the consequences of cyberbullying that young people experience are long lasting and significant. This debate has, in part, been fuelled by research with education practitioners. For example, 25 % of the high school teachers asked thought that cyberbullying did not have lasting consequences but rather prepared students for later life (Stauffer, Heath, Coyne, & Ferrin, 2012). Similarly, trainee teachers also thought that the consequences of cyberbullying were less than face-to-face bullying (Craig, Bell, & Leschied, 2011).

One reason which may account for why some teachers believe that cyberbullying is less likely to have long-term consequences is because they believe that children and young people have a 'moral compass' (Betts & Spenser, 2015). Through a series of focus groups, teachers talked about how they believed that children and young people had a 'moral compass' that protects them from experiences that they encounter in the digital world. The reason why some teachers believe that a 'moral compass' exists is that they recognise that not all young people who use technology experience the adverse effects associated with it and, as such, must be doing something to protect themselves.

Regardless of the teachers' perceptions of the consequences associated with involvement in cyberbullying for young people, there is a wealth of studies that have reported that young people experience adjustment consequences. However, it is vital to appreciate that much of the existing research literature examining the consequences of cyberbullying that has been conducted to date is cross-sectional in nature. Together, these cross-sectional studies provide evidence of associations between variables but, because they contain only a single assessment point, it is not possible to establish causality. Therefore, in other words, it is not possible to determine whether the consequences occur before or after an individual has experienced cyberbullying. In order to be able to answer this question, future research is needed that includes multiple assessment points to explore the extent to which cyberbullying predicts changes in adjustment. By adopting such longitudinal designs, it would be possible to infer causality in the relationship between cyberbullying and psychosocial adjustment. More recently, some studies have adopted a longitudinal approach to examining the psychosocial consequences of cyberbullying. However, as noted in Chaps. 2 and 3, it is important to note that these studies have used different conceptualisations of cyberbullying and different assessment methods. Therefore, it is appropriate to question the extent to which comparisons can be made across these studies. Further, Law, Shapka, Hymel, Olson, and Waterhouse (2012) argue that it is hard to draw firm conclusions about the impact of involvement in cyberbullying for psychosocial adjustment because of the limitations associated with how cyberbullying has been assessed.

Finally, as with many studies examining bullying that use self-report, many of the studies examining cyberbullying and adjustment are limited by common method variance. Common method variance also referred to as shared method variance occurs when the informant for predictor and outcome variables are the same (Lindell & Whitney, 2001). The effect of this is that the correlation coefficients are artificially higher than they would be if different informants were used for the predictor and outcome variables. Hawker and Boulton's (2000) seminal meta-analysis on the outcomes of face-to-face bullying clearly illustrates the effect of shared method variance on correlation coefficients. For example, the mean effect size of the association between peer victimisation and depression was $r=.29$ without shared method variance and was $r=.45$ with shared method variance.

In spite of the questions about whether the consequences of involvement in cyberbullying are long lasting and the methodological issues associated with the previous research, the meta-analysis of existing literature undertaken by Kowalski, Giumetti, Schroeder, and Lattanner (2014) identifies a number of consistent associations. For example, experiencing cyberbullying is associated with higher levels of stress, suicidal ideation, depression, anxiety, loneliness, somatic symptoms, conduct and emotional problems, drug and alcohol use, and reduced life satisfaction, self-esteem, and prosocial behaviours. Kowalski et al. note that there was no significant association between being the target of cyberbullying and academic achievement. Being a perpetrator of cyberbullying is associated with drug and alcohol use, anxiety, depression, lower life satisfaction, self-esteem, and academic achievement, and higher levels of loneliness. However, Kowalski et al. caution that the magnitude of these associations, identified in the meta-analysis, is small.

In summary, this chapter has presented some of the emerging evidence of the consequences of being involved in cyberbullying for both the target and the perpetrator. The current research suggests that the pattern of consequences vary according to the role that young people fulfil in cyberbullying. Many of the studies conducted to date, and reviewed in this chapter, are cross-sectional in nature meaning that the long-term consequences of involvement in cyberbullying remain unclear. Therefore, longitudinal research conducted over a number of years is needed to fully appreciate the consequences of being involved in cyberbullying. However, whilst these longer-term consequences of involvement in cyberbullying remain unclear, there is some emerging empirical evidence that the young people who are most 'at risk' of negative consequences are those who fulfil both the perpetrator and target role in cyberbullying (Gradinger et al., 2009). Gradinger et al. reported that those people most at risk of general poor adjustment assessed as high reactive and instrumental aggression, depressive symptoms, and somatic symptoms were those who fulfilled the perpetrator/target role.

REFERENCES

Abu-Hilal, M. M. (2000). A structural model of attitudes towards school subjects, academic aspiration, and achievement. *Education Psychology: An International Journal of Experimental Educational Psychology, 20,* 75–84.

Accordino, D. B., & Accordino, M. P. (2011). An exploratory study of face-to-face and cyberbullying in sixth grade students. *American Secondary Education, 40,* 14–30.

Álvarez-García, D., Núñez Pérez, J. C., Dobarro González, A., & Rodríguez Pérez, C. (2015). Risk factors associated with cybervictimization in adolescence. *International Journal of Clinical Health Psychology, 15,* 226–235.

Bannink, R., Broeren, S., Van de Looij-Jansen, P. M., de Waart, F. G., & Raat, H. (2014). Cyber and traditional bullying victimization as a risk factor for mental health problems and suicidal ideation in adolescents. *PLOS ONE, 9,* e94026.

Barlett, C. P., & Gentile, D. A. (2012). Attacking others online: The formation of cyberbullying in late adolescence. *Psychology of Popular Media Culture, 1,* 123–135.

Bauman, S., & Newman, M. L. (2013). Testing assumptions about cyberbullying: Perceived distress associated with acts of conventional and cyber bullying. *Psychology of Violence, 3,* 27–38.

Bayar, Y., & Ucanok, Z. (2012). School social climate and generalized peer perception in traditional and cyberbullying status. *Educational Studies: Theory & Practice, 12,* 2352–2358.

Berkelaar, B. L., & Buzzanell, P. M. (2014). Cybervetting, person-environment fit, and personnel selection: Employers' surveillance and sensemaking of job applicants' online information. *Journal of Applied Communication Research, 42,* 456–476.

Beran, T. N., Rinaldi, C., Bickham, D. S., & Rich, M. (2012). Evidence for the need to support adolescents dealing with harassment and cyber-harassment: Prevalence, progression, and impact. *School Psychology International, 33,* 562–576.

Betts, L. R., & Spenser, K. A. (2015). "A large can of worms": Teachers' perceptions of young people's experiences using technology. *International Journal of Cyber Behavior, Psychology and Learning, 5,* 15–29.

Borgia, L. G., & Myers, J. J. (2010). Cyber safety and children's literature: A good match for creating classroom communities. *Illinois Reading Council Journal, 38,* 29–34.

Calvete, E., Orue, I., Estévez, A., Villardón, L., & Padilla, P. (2010). Cyberbullying in adolescents: Modalities and aggressors' profile. *Computers in Human Behavior, 26,* 1128–1135.

Campbell, M. A., Slee, P. T., Spears, B., Butler, S., & Kift, S. (2013). Do cyberbullies suffer too? Cyberbullies' perceptions of the harm they cause to others and to their own mental health. *School Psychology International, 34,* 613–629.

Cénat, J. M., Hébert, M., Blais, M., Lavoie, F., Guerrier, M., & Derivois, D. (2014). Cyberbullying, psychological distress and self-esteem among youth in Quebec schools. *Journal of Affective Disorders, 169,* 7–9.

Clark, L. A., & Roberts, S. J. (2010). Employer's use of social networking sites: A socially irresponsible practice. *Journal of Business Ethics, 95,* 507–525.

Craig, K., Bell, D., & Leschied, A. (2011). Pre-service teachers' knowledge and attitudes regarding school-based bullying. *Canadian Journal of Education, 34,* 21–33.

Cross, D., Lester, L., & Barnes, A. (2015). A longitudinal study of the social and emotional predictors and consequences of cyber and traditional bullying victimisation. *International Journal of Public Health, 60,* 207–217.

Crosslin, K., & Crosslin, M. (2014). Cyberbullying at a Texas University—A mixed methods approach to examining online aggression. *Texas Public Health Journal, 66,* 26–31.

Cuadrado-Gordillo, I., & Fernández-Antelo, I. (2014). Cyberspace as a generator of changes in the aggressive-victim role. *Computers in Human Behavior, 36,* 225–233.

Dempsey, A. G., Sulkowski, M. L., Nichols, R., & Storch, E. A. (2009). Differences between peer victimization in cyber and physical settings and associated psychosocial adjustment in early adolescence. *Psychology in the Schools, 46,* 962–972.

DeSmet, A., Deforche, B., Hublet, A., Tanghe, A., Stremersch, E., & De Bourdeaudhuji, I. (2014). Traditional and cyberbullying victimization as correlates of psychosocial distress and barriers to a healthy lifestyle among severely obese adolescents—A matched case-control study on prevalence rates from a cross-sectional study. *BMC Public Health, 14,* 224.

Didden, R., Scholte, R. H. J., Korzilius, H., De Moor, J. M. H., Vermeulen, A., O'Reilly, M., … Lancioni, G. E. (2009). Cyberbullying among students with intellectual and developmental disability in special education settings. *Developmental Neurorehabilitation, 12,* 146–151.

Dooley, J. J., Pyżalski, J., & Cross, D. (2009). Cyberbullying versus face-to-face bullying: A theoretical and conceptual review. *Zeitschrift für Psychologie/Journal of Psychology, 217,* 182–188.

Festl, R., & Quandt, T. (2013). Social relations and cyberbullying: The influence of individual and structural attributes on victimization and perpetration via the internet. *Human Communication Research, 39,* 101–126.

Frey, K. S., Pearson, C. R., & Cohen, D. (2015). Revenge is seductive, if not sweet: Why friends *matter* for prevention efforts. *Journal of Applied Developmental Psychology, 37,* 25–35.

Gámez-Guadix, M., Gini, G., & Calvete, E. (2015). Stability of cyberbuyllying victimization among adolescents: Prevalence and association with bully-victim status and psychosocial adjustment. *Computers in Human Behavior, 53,* 140–148.

Giumetti, G. W., Hatfield, A. L., Scisco, J. L., Schroeder, A. N., Muth, E. R., & Kowalski, R. M. (2013). What a rude email! Examining the differential effects of incivility versus support on mood, energy, engagement, and performance in an online context. *Journal of Occupational Health Psychology, 18,* 297–309.

Goebert, D., Else, I., Matsu, C., Chung-Do, J., & Chang, J. Y. (2011). The impact of cyberbullying on substance use and mental health in a multiethnic sample. *Maternal and Child Health Journal, 15,* 1282–1286.

Gradinger, P., Strochmeier, D., & Spiel, C. (2009). Traditional bullying and cyberbullying: Identification of risk groups for adjustment problems. *Zeitschrift für Psychologie/Journal of Psychology, 217,* 205–213.

Hawker, D. S. J., & Boulton, M. J. (2000). Twenty years' research on peer victimization and psychosocial maladjustment: A meta-analytic review of cross-sectional studies. *Journal of Child Psychology and Psychiatry, and Allied Disciplines, 41,* 441–455.

Hinduja, S., & Patchin, J. W. (2010). Bullying, cyberbullying, and suicide. *Archives of Suicide Research, 14,* 206–221.

Imamura, A., Nishida, A., Nakazawa, N., Shimodera, S., Tanaka, G., Kinoshita, H., … & Okazaki, Y. (2009). Effects of cellular phone email use on the mental health of junior high school students in Japan. *Psychiatry and Clinical Neurosciences, 63,* 703.

Jackson, C. L., & Cohen, R. (2012). Childhood victimization: Modeling the relation between classroom victimization, cyber victimization, and psychosocial functioning. *Psychology of Popular Media, 1,* 254–269.

Jang, H., Song, J., & Kim, R. (2014). Does the offline bully-victimization influence cyberbullying behavior among youths? Application of general strain theory. *Computers in Human Behavior, 31,* 85–93.

Juvonen, J., & Gross, E. F. (2008). Extending the school grounds?—Bullying experiences in cyberspace. *Journal of School Health, 78,* 496–505.

Katzer, C., Fetchenhauer, D., & Belschak, F. (2009). Cyberbullying: Who are the victims? A comparison of victimization in internet chatrooms and victimization in school. *Journal of Media Psychology, 21,* 25–36.

Kite, S. L., Gable, R., & Filippelli, L. (2010). Assessing middle school students' knowledge of conduct and consequences and their behaviours regarding the use of social networking sites. *The Clearing House, 83,* 158–163.

König, A., Gollwitzer, M., & Steffgen, G. (2010). Cyberbullying as an act of revenge? *Australian Journal of Guidance & Counselling, 20,* 210–224.

Kowalski, R. M., Giumetti, G. W., Schroeder, A. N., & Lattanner, M. R. (2014). Bulling in the digital age: A critical review and meta-analysis of cyberbullying research among youth. *Psychological Bulletin, 140,* 1073–1137.

Kubiszewksi, V., Fontaine, R., Potard, C., & Auzoult, L. (2015). Does cyberbul-lying overlap with school bullying when taking modality of involvement into account? *Computers in Human Behavior, 43*, 49–57.

Lam, L. T., Cheng, Z., & Liu, X. (2013). Violent online games exposure and cyberbullying/victimization among adolescents. *Cyberpsychology, Behavior, and Social Networking, 16*, 159–164.

Landoll, R. R., La Greca, A. M., Lai, B. S., Chan, S. F., & Herge, W. M. (2015). Cyber victimization by peers: Prospective associations with adolescent social anxiety and depressive symptoms. *Journal of Adolescence, 42*, 77–86.

Law, D. M., Shapka, J. D., Hymel, S., Olson, B. F., & Waterhouse, T. (2012). The changing face of bullying: An empirical comparison between traditional and internet bullying and victimization. *Computers in Human Behavior, 28*, 226–232.

Li, Q. (2007). Bullying in the new playground: Research into cyberbullying and cyber victimization. *Australasian Journal of Educational Technology, 23*, 435–454.

Lindell, M. K., & Whitney, D. J. (2001). Accounting for common method vari-ance in cross-sectional research designs. *Journal of Applied Psychology, 86*, 114–121.

Litwiller, B. J., & Brausch, A. M. (2013). Cyber bullying and physical bullying in adolescent suicide: The role of violent behaviour and substance use. *Journal of Youth and Adolescence, 42*, 675–684.

Lonigro, A., Schneider, B. H., Laghi, F., Baiocco, R., Pallini, S., & Brunner, T. (2015). Is cyberbullying related to trait or state anger? *Child Psychiatry & Human Development, 46*, 445–454.

Machmutow, K., Perren, S., Sticca, F., & Alsaker, F. D. (2012). Peer victimisation and depressive symptoms: Can specific coping strategies buffer the negative impact of cybervictimisation. *Emotional and Behavioral Difficulties, 17*, 403–420.

Marr, N., & Field, T. (2001). *Bullycide: Death at play time.* Success Unlimited Didcot, Oxfordshire.

McDermott, M. (2012). *The relationship between cyberbullying and depression in adolescents.* Maters thesis, Eastern Illinois University, Charleston, IL.

Nixon, C. L. (2014). Current perspectives: The impact of cyberbullying on ado-lescent health. *Adolescent Health, Medicine and Therapeutics, 5*, 143–158.

O'Keeffe, G. W., Clarke-Pearson, K., & Council on Communication and Media. (2011). Clinical report—The impact of social media on children, adolescents, and families. *Paediatrics, 127*, 800–804.

Ortega, R., Elipe, P., Moran-Merchán, J. A., Genta, M. L., Brighi, A., Guraini, A., ... Tippett, A. (2009). The emotional impact of bullying and cyberbullying on victims: A European cross-national study. *Aggressive Behavior, 38*, 342–356.

Patchin, J. W., & Hinduja, S. (2006). Bullies move beyond the schoolyard: A preliminary look at cyberbullying. *Youth Violence and Juvenile Justice, 4,* 148–169.

Patchin, J. W., & Hinduja, S. (2010). Changes in adolescent online social networking behaviors from 2006 to 2009. *Computers in Human Behavior, 26,* 1818–1821.

Pendergrass, W., & Wright, M. (2014). Cyberbullied to death: An analysis of victims taken from recent events. *Issues in Information Sciences, 15,* 132–140.

Perren, S., Dooley, J., Shaw, T., & Cross, D. (2010). Bullying in school and cyberspace: Associations with depressive symptoms in Swiss and Australian adolescents. *Child and Adolescent Psychiatry and Mental Health, 4,* 28.

Price, M., Chin, M. A., Higa-McMillan, C., Kim, S., & Frueh, B. C. (2013). Prevalence and internalizing problems of ethnoracially diverse victims of traditional and cyber bullying. *School Mental Health, 5,* 183–191.

Pyzalski, J. (2012). From cyberbullying to electronic aggression: Typology of the phenomenon. *Emotional and Behavioural Difficulties, 17,* 305–317.

Raskauskas, J., & Stoltz, A. D. (2007). Involvement in traditional and electronic bullying among adolescents. *Developmental Psychology, 43,* 564–575.

Reeckman, B., & Cannard, L. (2009). Cyberbullying: A TAFE perspective. *Youth Studies Australia, 28,* 41–49.

Rivituso, J. (2014). Cyberbullying victimization among college students: An interpretive phenomenological analysis. *Journal of Information Systems Education, 25,* 71–75.

Rodkin, P. C., & Fischer, K. (2012). Cyberbullying from psychological and legal perspectives. *Missouri Law Review, 77,* 619–640.

Rosen, J. (2012). The right to be forgotten. *Stanford Law Review Online, 64,* 88–92.

Rotenberg, K. J. (1994). Loneliness and interpersonal trust. *Journal of Social and Clinical Psychology, 13,* 152–173.

Sampasa-Kanyinga, H., Roumeliotis, P., Farrow, C. V., & Shi, Y. F. (2014). Breakfast skipping is associated with cyberbullying and school bullying victimization. A school-based cross-sectional study. *Appetite, 79,* 76–82.

Sampasa-Kanyinga, H., Roumeliotis, P., & Xu, H. (2014). Associations between cyberbullying and school bullying victimization and suicidal ideation, plans and attempts among Canadian schoolchildren. *PloS ONE, 9*(7), e102145.

Selkie, E. M., Kota, R., Chan, Y.-F., & Moreno, M. (2015). Cyberbullying, depression, and problem alcohol use in female college students: A multisite study. *Cyberpsychology, Behavior, and Social Networking, 18,* 79–86.

Sinclair, K. O., Bauman, S., Poteat, P., Boenig, B., & Russell, S. T. (2012). Cyber and bias-based harassment: Associations with academic, substance use, and mental health problems. *Journal of Adolescent Health, 50,* 521–523.

Sourander, A., Klomek, A. B., Ikonen, M., Lindroos, J., Luntamo, T., Koskelainen, M., ... Helenius, H. (2010). Psychosocial risk factors associated with cyberbullying among adolescents: A population based study. *Achieves of General Psychiatry, 67,* 720–728.

Spears, B., Slee, P., Owens, L., & Johnson, B. (2009). Behind the scenes and screens: Insights into the human dimension of covert and cyberbullying. *Zeitschrift für Psychologie/Journal of Psychology, 217,* 189–196.

Spenser, K. A., & Betts, L. R. (2014, May). "People think it's a harmless joke when really it could be hurting someone": Young people's experiences of cyber bullying. Poster presented at the *British Psychological Society Annual Conference,* International Convention Centre, Birmingham.

Stauffer, S., Heath, M. A., Coyne, S. M., & Ferrin, S. (2012). High school teachers' perceptions of cyberbullying prevention and intervention strategies. *Psychology in the Schools, 49,* 353–367.

Varjas, K., Talley, J., Meyers, J., Parris, L., & Cutts, H. (2010). High school students' perceptions of motivations for cyberbullying: An exploratory study. *Western Journal of Emergency Medicine, 11,* 269–273.

West, D. (2015). An investigation into the prevalence of cyberbullying among students aged 16–19 in post-compulsory education. *Research in Post-Compulsory Education, 20,* 96–112.

Wright, M. F., & Li, Y. (2013). Normative beliefs about aggression and cyber aggression among young adults: A longitudinal investigation. *Aggressive Behavior, 39,* 161–170.

Ybarra, M. L., Diener-West, M., & Leaf, P. J. (2007). Examining the overlap in internet harassment and school bullying: Implications for school intervention. *Journal of Adolescent Health, 41,* S42–S50.

CHAPTER 6

What Can Be Done About Cyberbullying

Abstract Concern over the high prevalence rates of cyberbullying and the consequences associated with involvement in cyberbullying has prompted some researchers and practitioners to develop interventions designed to tackle cyberbullying. Some of the current interventions use technology to educate young people about appropriate digital behaviour, whereas other interventions are designed to enhance young people's coping skills. However, one complexity is who is responsible for addressing young people's involvement in cyberbullying, and researchers and practitioners have questioned the appropriateness of current legislation as a mechanism to tackle cyberbullying. This chapter will provide an account of some of the interventions designed to tackle cyberbullying and the existing legislation.

Keywords Cyberbullying • Anti-bullying interventions • Legislation • Disclosure

Whilst it has been suggested that cyberbullying is an unintended consequence of young people's technology use (Tokunaga, 2010), it is important to acknowledge that we live in a society where technology use is increasing. Further, there is also the increasing drive for companies and organisations to become 'digital by default' meaning that the prominence of technology is likely to continue to increase. Technology use can, of course, offer a number of benefits for children and young people. For

© The Editor(s) (if applicable) and The Author(s) 2016   103
L.R. Betts, *Cyberbullying*, DOI 10.1057/978-1-137-50009-0_6

example, 10- to 18-year-olds who use the Internet at home have higher reading scores on standardised tests compared to those who do not access the Internet at home (Jackson et al., 2006). Jackson et al. attribute their findings to the amount of text on webpages and argue that those young people who spend more time online develop their reading skills as a result of the text they encounter.

Despite the many benefits associated with technology use, it is important to recognise, as argued elsewhere throughout this book, that cyberbullying is a pervasive and insidious experience for many young people. Approximately, half of the young people asked by Ackers (2012) recognised that potentially anyone is at risk of becoming the target of cyberbullying. However, the same group of participants also said that they would be unlikely to disclose cyberbullying because of fear, embarrassment, or the belief that they will make the situation worse. Similarly, Juvonen and Gross (2008) reported that 90% of the 12- to 17-year-olds that had experienced cyberbullying said that they would not tell anyone about their experiences. When asked why the young people would not disclose their experiences, 50% said that it was because they thought that they should learn to deal with it and 31% said that they did not tell anyone because they were worried that their parents would block or limit their access to technology. The most commonly used prevention tactics reported by this group of young people was to block the screen name of the perpetrator or to change their own screen name.

A recent study with undergraduate students found that only 54% of those who experienced cyberbullying would disclose their experiences to someone else (Paullet & Pinchot, 2014). Of those that did tell someone about their experiences, 68% reported telling a friend, 21% a counsellor, and 16% their parents. However, only 37% of those who disclosed their experiences of cyberbullying reported that they had received any help to deal with the cyberbullying. Similarly, in a study with junior high school students, 64.1% of the sample thought that teachers did something about cyberbullying (Li, 2006). Consequently, researchers and practitioners have begun to explore methods of addressing cyberbullying. Broadly, these methods include developing interventions to support targets and perpetrators and changes to legislation and laws under which acts of cyberbullying fall both of which will be explored in this chapter. Finally, the chapter will end by drawing together some of the common themes with regard to the practicalities of implementing the recommended interventions and legal aspects with regard to cyberbullying.

6.1 INTERVENTIONS

The face-to-face bullying literature has advocated a wide range, and varied number, of interventions to tackle bullying. Some of the interventions are designed to work at the whole school level, whereas others are designed to work at the classroom level or exclusively with those directly involved with a bullying episode. It has been suggested that if schools tackle face-to-face bullying, this will also impact on levels of cyberbullying (Olweus, 2012). However, despite the wealth of interventions designed to address face-to-face bullying, the evidence of their success in reducing face-to-face bullying or enhancing the well-being of those involved in bullying has been found to be somewhat limited. For example, a meta-analysis undertaken on 16 studies conducted from 1980 to 2004 which included over 15,000 participants reported that the interventions impacted on only a third of the variables in a positive way (Merrell, Gueldner, Ross, & Isava, 2008). The meta-analysis also revealed that there was little evidence of 'meaningful change' as a result of the intervention, either positive or negative. Consequently, the effectiveness of interventions designed to tackle face-to-face bullying appear to be limited. However, Merrell et al. argued that, despite finding only limited evidence of positive outcomes of the interventions that they reviewed, the interventions did serve an important role in raising awareness of bullying, changing attitudes, and self-perceptions rather than changing bullying behaviours per se.

As with face-to-face bullying, a range of interventions have been developed to support individuals who experience cyberbullying, some of these interventions are specifically designed to be delivered through technology, whereas other interventions rely less on technology for their delivery. Key to the success of any of the interventions that have been developed and utilised is understanding young people's perceptions of cyberbullying (Barlett, 2015). Specifically, understanding why individuals engage in such behaviours may enable researchers and practitioners to develop strategies to modify this behaviour.

One example of an intervention using technology to tackle cyberbullying is Online Pestkoppenstoppen (stop bullies online/stop online bullies, Jacobs, Völlink, Dehue, & Lechner, 2014). The intervention is designed for 12- to 15-year-olds and comprises a fully automated web based bespoke programme that involves 3 advice sessions undertaken over 3 months to promote the development of coping skills in targets of cyberbullying. The first session teaches participants about how their thoughts may impact on cyberbullying, how to recognise and disrupt irrational thoughts, and how to form rationale thoughts. The second session discusses how cyberbullying can occur, how behaviour can influence cyberbullying, and how to cope with cyberbullying. Session three gives young people feedback on their skills using technology and encourages them to further develop their skills so that they use technology safely. Throughout the intervention, the participating young people receive personalised feedback based on their personality, self-efficacy, coping styles, and irrational thoughts. The researchers who developed the intervention have reported that the intervention appears to be effective in developing young people's coping skills (Jacobs et al., 2014).

Although additional evaluation concerning the effectiveness of the newly developed Pestkoppenstoppen is required, it is likely that developing young people's coping styles in response to cyberbullying may be effective to ameliorate some of the consequences of experiencing cyberbullying. Research evidence suggests that the coping style young people adopt in the face of cyberbullying can impact on their well-being (Völlink, Bolman, Dehue, & Jacobs, 2013). Adopting a cyber-specific depressive coping style, when experiencing cyberbullying, is predictive of depressive feelings and health complaints in 11- to 12-year-olds. Conversely, adopting a problem solving approach to cyberbullying is more likely to be endorsed by non-victims of cyberbullying. Therefore, developing young people's coping styles may go some way to reduce some of the negative impacts of cyberbullying, such as those outlined in Chap. 5.

In support of developing young people's coping skills, as advocated by the Pestkoppenstoppen programme, a number of studies have examined the coping mechanisms that young people use when they experience cyberbullying. For example, Machackova, Cerna, Sevcikova, Dedkova, and Daneback (2013) examined the coping strategies and the effectiveness of these strategies used by 12- to 18-year-olds when they encounter cyberbullying. The young people reported using more than one strategy, with targets of cyberbullying reporting blocking contacts, seeking support, or ignoring the perpetrator as a way of dealing with cyberbullying. However, these strategies were regarded as less effective than when they were used to cope with Internet harassment. The most common strategies for dealing with cyberbullying were depreciating the perpetrator, talking to someone, and avoiding thinking about the incident. The most frequently used cognitive strategy was focusing attention on something else. Avoiding the perpetrator of cyberbullying was also a common strategy for dealing with cyberbullying, with confrontation used about half of the time and retaliation used infrequently. Most of the technology strategies were regarded as moderately useful and the strategies that were reported as helpful for stopping cyberbullying were to implement technological methods, avoid the site, and seek support.

The coping strategies of younger children who experience cyberbullying have also been explored (Völlink et al., 2013). Völlink et al. examined the coping strategies of 11- to 12-year-olds and reported that targets of cyberbullying cope differently from those who are perpetrator/targets and those not involved in cyberbullying. Targets of cyberbullying reported using more emotion-focused coping strategies such as getting angry or irritated when they encountered daily stressors. However, adopting an emotional expressive coping style in daily life resulted in more cyber-specific depressive/emotional coping styles when an individual encountered cyberbullying. This depressive/emotional coping style was typified by feelings of distress, powerlessness, anger, and a reluctance to do anything about the cyberbullying. Adopting this depressive/emotional coping style resulted in the young people experiencing more depressive feelings and health complaints. On the other hand, those young people who were not targets of cyberbullying were more likely to see cyberbullying as something that was less rigid, something that could be changed, and were more likely to adopt problem solving techniques.

More recently, Whittaker and Kowalski (2015) asked university students to report the strategies that they used to cope when they experienced cyberbullying. The most frequent strategies reported by those who had experienced cyberbullying included blocking the perpetrator on social media (34.1%), reporting the cyberbullying (31.8%), and asking the person to stop (29.5%). Some of the participants also reported that they collected evidence of what was happening to them (18.2%) and, consistent with previous findings, some targets of cyberbullying reported that they would cyberbully the perpetrator (13.6%). Whittaker and Kowalski also examined the participants' perceptions of what they thought others would do when they experienced cyberbullying. The most frequently endorsed responses were: doing nothing (25%), asking the perpetrator to stop (15.9%), and retaliating against the perpetrator by cyberbullying them back (11.4%).

Another example of an intervention designed to tackle cyberbullying is Cyberprogram 2.0 (Garaigordobil & Marinez-Valderrey, 2015). The programme, which was developed with 13- to 15-year-olds from Spain, consists of 19 one-hour sessions. These sessions comprise four types of activities: identifying and conceptualising bullying/cyberbullying and the associated roles, analysing the consequences for those in the various roles, developing coping strategies, and developing other positive skills. The weekly sessions are facilitated by an adult and involve reflective discussion activities, guided discussion activities, role plays, brainstorming, and case studies. The success of the programme was evidenced by a reduction in cyberbullying and bullying behaviours and experiences and an increase in empathy in the young people who undertook the programme compared to the control group.

The ViSC anti-bullying policy is part of the Austrian national plan to tackle bullying. The programme was developed as a preventative programme that aims to reduce bullying and aggressive behaviours, and foster social intercultural competencies in schools (Gardinger, Yanagida, Strohmeier, & Spiel, 2015). The programme is targeted at secondary school age children and is implemented over a year and then continues indefinitely as part of the school ethos. Initially, teachers are the primary targets for change and the programme covers prevention and intervention. In subsequent stages of the programme, students and teachers work together to bring about change in the school. Teachers are also trained to recognise bullying, tackle bullying, and implement preventative measures at the school and class level. Students are also taught about how to take responsibility for what happens in their class. Initially, students work together to discuss bullying prevention and how to prevent aggressive behaviour and then work together to achieve a common goal and practise their social skills. However, unlike the other interventions discussed so far in this chapter, the ViSC intervention does not tackle bullying or cyberbullying per se but rather tries to promote an environment where these behaviours are less likely to occur. Gradinger et al. evaluated the effectiveness of ViSC over time and reported that, compared to the intervention group, the control group who did not experience the intervention experienced an increase in cyberbullying, whereas the intervention group experienced a reduction in cyberbullying.

Interventions have also been developed that target younger children's experience of cyberbullying. For example, Toshack and Colmar (2012) developed and evaluated an intervention with a group of primary school aged girls from Australia. The intervention comprises six sessions that discuss: (1) what is cyberbullying, (2) how to notice cyberbullying, (3) Internet safety, (4) staying engaged at school if you are being cyberbullied, (5) how to help others, and (6) review. The sessions involve a mixture of interactive activities, worksheets, quizzes, group discussions, and case studies to facilitate learning. Post intervention, Toshack and Colmar reported that the participants had a greater knowledge of cyberbullying and appropriate safety strategies.

Although not a specific form of an intervention, Borgia and Myers (2010) advocate the use of fiction as a mechanism for engaging young people with the issues associated with cyberbullying. Specifically, Borgia and Myers review a list of books (e.g., *Beacon Street Girls: Just Kidding* by Bryant, 2009) that explicitly deal with issues aligned to cyberbullying and argue that these books could be used as the catalyst for conversations around cyberbullying. Whilst the cyberbullying interventions discussed so far in the chapter have been found in some studies to be effective in reducing cyberbullying in the intervention group compared to the control group, further research is needed to examine whether these effects are sustained over longer periods of time. Further, it is also important to consider whether the interventions have differential effects according to the role an individual plays within cyberbullying to ensure that the interventions are as effective as possible and targeted appropriately.

In addition to the specific interventions previously discussed, that have tackled cyberbullying through focusing either directly on cyberbullying or on associated behaviours, interventions can also be developed to address and enhance young people's digital technology skills. Developing and enhancing young people's digital citizenship, media literacy, and netiquette through education may prompt young people to develop a greater awareness of appropriate behaviour and the consequences of inappropriate behaviour, and, as such, may reduce cyberbullying. The rationale for fostering such skills is that empirical evidence suggests that those young people who engage in 'risky' behaviour online are more likely to experience cyberbullying (Erdur-Baker, 2010). Consequently, Bhat, Chang, and Linscott (2010) proposed a number of recommendations with regard to enhancing young people's skill set and awareness which include

- providing definitions of cyberbullying and the associated behaviours,
- enhancing knowledge and understanding of media used to cyberbully,
- explaining the various cyberbullying roles,
- creating expectations to stay safe online and developing strategies for each platform,

- clarifying what individuals should do if they experience cyberbullying (e.g., screen shots, printing evidence, speaking to a trusted adult, avoiding retaliation),
- giving examples of behaviours that reduce cyberbullying,
- understanding the effects of cyberbullying,
- developing reporting procedures, and
- outlining the consequences for those who engage in cyberbullying.

Similar to enhancing young people's digital literacy, some researchers have proposed specific guidelines that young people should follow when using digital technology as a way of reducing the likelihood of experiencing cyberbullying. For example, Wolfsberg (2006) suggests that young people who experience cyberbullying should avoid engaging with the perpetrator of cyberbullying, keep records of everything, change their screen name, avoid disclosing personal information, contact their service provider, think before they send messages to the perpetrator, involve their parents and teachers, and take action. Similarly, Raskauskas and Stoltz (2007) advocate that young people who experience cyberbullying should take cyber harassment seriously, if the harassment includes physical threats, then they should notify the police, avoid disclosing personal contact information to others, refrain from replying to cyberbullying messages, block the sender, save messages that contain cyberbullying and if appropriate forwarding them to the Internet service provider, and when witnessing cyberbullying, speak out. Together, these recommendations are aligned to the calls to enhance young people's digital literacy skills because they specifically outline what young people should do when using digital technology.

In addition to enhancing young people's digital technology skills, other areas which cyberbullying interventions could focus on are developing moral behaviour and empathy in the digital environment. Research evidence has suggested that moral disengagement is associated with being a perpetrator of cyberbullying (Lazuras, Barkouskis, Ourda, & Tsorbatzoudis, 2013). Further, redefining the normative behaviour of young people's peer group in the digital world may also be a mechanism to address cyberbullying. Specifically, there is evidence that for some peer groups, cyberbullying and aggression are normative in their interactions (Dehue, Bolman, & Völlink, 2008; Lazuras et al., 2013). Consequently, some peer groups may be engaging in cyberbullying and aggression without recognising the consequences of their actions. Aligned to this recommendation, Pabian and Vandebosch (2014) advocate developing interventions that have the overarching aim of enhancing young people's empathy. In addition to developing empathy, the authors argued that teaching young people how to resist negative peer pressure and using peers who have high social status as educators of cyberbullying could offer alternative solutions for tackling cyberbullying.

Another, perhaps more controversial mechanism for dealing with cyberbullying is limiting young people's access to digital technology. Limiting young people's access to technology would be consistent with the time displacement hypothesis outlined by Espinosa and Clemente (2013). According to this hypothesis, the amount of time young people spend online prevents them from engaging in other face-to-face social activities which, in turn, could negatively impact on their cognitive development. Consequently, by limiting the amount of time young people spend online, this gives them the opportunity to enhance their cognitive skill set. Empirical support for this hypothesis includes work by Erdur-Baker (2010) which reports that spending more time using technology is a significant predictor of being the target of cyberbullying. Similarly, Mark and Ratliffe (2011) reported that time spent online predicted the likelihood with which middle-school children were targets and perpetrators of cyberbullying: Spending more time online predicted greater involvement in cyberbullying. However, the extent to which these findings can be solely attributed to the amount of time a young person spends online can be questioned. Specifically, it may be the nature of the activities that the young people engage in when using technology which may place them at greater risk of involvement in cyberbullying rather than the time they spend using technology per se. Spending more time online may also increase the probability with which young people encounter or engage in cyberbullying because they are in the environment for a greater length of time.

Of course, if limiting young people's access to technology was used as a strategy to deal with cyberbullying, this would reinforce their beliefs that if they disclose experiences of cyberbullying, they would have their access to technology removed (Thomas, 2006) and, as such, may prevent them from disclosing their experiences. Aside from the potential exclusion from society that may occur if young people's technology use is limited, many young people report that they will not disclose their experiences of cyberbullying because they fear that their access to technology will be removed (Mishna, Saini, & Solomon, 2009). Further, whilst young people report that they most frequently tell their peers and parents about their experiences, young people thought that peers and adults were not effective in reducing cyberbullying (Holfeld & Grabe, 2012).

Tokunaga (2010) suggests that the ambiguity surrounding who regulates negative behaviour when using technology is a unique feature of cyberbullying. Specifically, Tokunaga argues that in comparison to face-to-face bullying, where school personnel often intervene, there is a lack of consensus with regard to who regulates cyberbullying. On the other hand, Campbell (2011) believes that schools should take an active role in tackling cyberbullying. However, schools need to be mindful of their legal responsibilities, the wider community context, and their moral responsibilities when responding to cyberbullying. Campbell states that it is the school's responsibility to address cyberbullying because they are responsible for the safety of their pupils and cyberbullying likely impacts on behaviour in school. However, these moral and legal responsibilities that schools have for ensuring the children's safety can come into conflict with the right for freedom of speech (Brydolf, 2007). Further, from a practical point, as noted by Couvillon and Ilieva (2011), interventions developed and implemented by schools are likely to be able to target most of those engaged in the various roles of cyberbullying. Moreover, when cyberbullying causes disruption to the school environment or prevents a conducive learning environment, in America, schools can be prosecuted for not taking appropriate action (Lane, 2011).

Although many researchers have called for educational practitioners to be involved in the delivery of interventions and education on cyberbullying, it is important to acknowledge that cyberbullying is potentially a difficult topic for school personnel to manage (Couvillon & Ilieva, 2011). Ross (2013) also argues that school personnel may contribute to the continuation and perpetuation of bullying because of their behaviour. Specifically, if school personnel chose to ignore cyberbullying or not act following an incidence of cyberbullying, then they may be reinforcing cyberbullying and, as such, may inadvertently cause the behaviour to occur more frequently. Further, the ecology of the school may also influence the perceptions of the perpetrator, target, and their interactions (Kueny & Zirkel, 2012). Also, perceptions of students and school personnel may promote a school culture that varies between establishments with regard to how much cyberbullying is tolerated. Withstanding the arguments presented by Ross, some researchers have provided recommendations for how school administrators should tackle cyberbullying. For example, Simmons and Bynum (2014) recently recommended that school administrators should

- ensure that school policies are updated to include cyberbullying,
- integrate teaching on cyberbullying within the curriculum and provide appropriate lessons to young people and their parents,
- establish a school wide task force that is responsible for the development and implementation of cyberbullying interventions,
- develop appropriate working relationships surrounding cyberbullying with local police,
- foster and facilitate an environment within the school where young people feel able to report their experiences of cyberbullying to staff, and
- document all instances and reports of cyberbullying.

Similar to the approaches previously outlined, some researchers and practitioners have suggested that school staff should monitor young people for changes in their behaviour which may be associated with cyberbullying. Suggested behavioural changes for those who are the target of cyberbullying include suddenly stopping using technology, appearing anxious when receiving a message, seeming angry or depressed having used technology, avoiding going to school or out in general, an unwillingness to discuss activities they have engaged in using technology, and withdrawal from social situations (Diamanduros, Downs, & Jenkins, 2008). Conversely, perpetrators of cyberbullying may close screens when someone enters the room, use technology constantly, display high levels of upset if they cannot access technology, laugh excessively when using technology, avoid talking about what they are doing when using technology, and use multiple accounts or may not use their own account. Diamanduros et al. recommend that teachers should be made aware of these behavioural changes through training so that they can tackle the behaviour of their students, if appropriate.

Despite the many recommendations from the research literature that teachers and schools should implement interventions, that aim to reduce cyberbullying and ameliorate the consequences of cyberbullying, it is important to recognise that not all educational practitioners share this view. A recent study undertaken by Stauffer, Heath, Coyne, and Ferrin (2012), examining high school teachers' perceptions of cyberbullying, reported that under half of the teachers asked were in favour of implementing an anti-bullying policy within their school. However, the teachers did endorse increased parental involvement, education of the consequences of cyberbullying, and severity of the consequences of cyberbullying as mechanisms for tackling cyberbullying. Further, empirical evidence also reports that only 1% of young people would tell their teacher if they experienced cyberbullying (Aricak et al., 2008).

In addition to the debates about whether teachers should be responsible for the actions of young people, dealing with cyberbullying also poses challenges for teachers and educational practitioners because of the many educational advantages of using technology (Campbell, 2011). Campbell argues that policies which restrict access to technology may have the unintended consequence of limiting the learning and educational opportunities of young people. Further, whilst schools are responsible for creating a safe learning environment for their students, this potential impact of cyberbullying policies is limited because cyberbullying can happen at any time. Campbell likens a young person receiving a punishment for cyberbullying that has occurred out of school as akin to them receiving a punishment for violating a school policy at the weekend.

The lack of clarity over who is responsible for young people's behaviour online has prompted some to argue that parents/guardians need to be more aware of what their son(s)/daughter(s) are doing when they are online (e.g., Law et al., 2010). Law et al. reported that, of those 10- to 18-year-olds surveyed, those who had a computer in their bedroom were more likely to report engaging in online aggression. Further, the rationale for involving parents in tackling cyberbullying is strengthened by examining analysis of the Pew Internet American Life Survey. Sengupta and Chaudhuri (2011) found that 12- to 17-year-olds from America were 60% more likely to be the target of cyberbullying if their parents were unaware of their online activities. The strength of this research is that the analyses were conducted on a nationally representative sample. Consequently, empowering parents to support their children when using technology seems an appropriate way of addressing cyberbullying.

Whilst empowering parents to tackle cyberbullying, it is important to recognise that there is a paradox between digital technology and safety. Specifically, Keith and Martin (2005) argue that parents give young people mobile telephones and other portable devices so that they can be contacted by them as a means to making the young people feel safe. However, whilst this connectivity to parents may give a sense of safety, by giving young people technology, parents are potentially inadvertently putting them at risk of experiencing cyberbullying. To address this paradox, Keith and Martin suggest that parents should

- pay attention to how children are using technology;
- become more technology savvy;
- install content blockers;
- encourage young people to disclose bullying;
- limit the amount of time young people can use technology; and
- develop a family agreement that outlines when young people can go online and what they can do, how much time they can spend online, what the young person should do if they feel uncomfortable, and how stay safe, behave ethically, and be responsible.

Robinson (2013) argues that the responsibility of parents for teaching children about online safety begins when children first start using technology. According to Robinson, parents need to educate children about how to stay safe in the digital world and how to use technology responsibly. However, as Robinson recognises parents should aim to strike an appropriate balance between monitoring and over protection. Parents who engage in excessive monitoring of their children's behaviour may inadvertently limit their children's developmental opportunities when using technology. Of course, it may be beneficial for young people to experience some risk when using technology, as by doing so will allow them to develop the skills they need to stay safe online and also deal with more significant risks that they encounter.

Whilst parents/guardians may play an important role in addressing cyberbullying, the potential digital divide between the generations must be acknowledged. In particular, the younger generations are more technology savvy and the current generation has been exposed to technology more so than their parents. Therefore, it may be that for some young people, their parents are unaware of some of the capabilities and functions of technology which may, in turn, hinder their ability to monitor, respond, and support young people experiencing and engaging in cyberbullying. However, Bhat et al. (2010) argue that parents should take steps to reduce cyberbullying, including

- setting appropriate rules for technology use,
- understanding privacy settings,
- negotiating with young people how much parents can know about their online activities, and
- discussing appropriate behaviour online and the consequences of actions.

As outlined above, one of the ways that many researchers and practitioners have suggested that cyberbullying can be addressed is through ensuring that parents are aware of what their son/daughter does when using technology. The extent to which parents are aware of what young people do online can be questioned. For example, Kite, Gable, and Filippelli (2010) reported that 70% of the 7th and 8th grade children they asked thought that their parents knew what they did online. However, this compared to 53% of the sample saying that they thought that their friends' parents were aware of what they did online.

In response to the challenge of who is responsible for young people's behaviour in the digital world, it has been argued that whole school approaches that strengthen the links between schools and families should be implemented to tackle cyberbullying (e.g., Beale & Hall, 2007; Pearce, Cross, Monks, Waters, & Falconer, 2011). At the heart of these approaches should be a protective school environment and home-school-family partnerships that work towards building capacity for action against cyberbullying and a shared understanding amongst all stakeholders of proactive policies, procedures, and practices. Further, it has been suggested that schools should actively encourage parents to ensure that digital technology is in a 'public' space at home, and discuss Internet safety, responsible technology use, and cyberbullying with their son/daughter (Diamanduros et al., 2008).

Building on the home-school link, more recently, Papatraianou, Levine, and West (2014) proposed a conceptual framework that included contextual factors that drew on a range of environments that could be used to promote resilience in young people who experience cyberbullying. Central to the underpinning of this approach was the notion that cyberbullying could occur at any time, and, as such, a range of contexts were needed to be examined in order to address the issue. Specifically, Papatraianou et al. proposed five contexts:

1. *Personal*—this includes internal factors of the individual and the individual's predisposition, including previous experience, psychological factors, and biological factors;
2. *Home*—this context highlights the importance of family members, including siblings, parents, and the family's social network. In addition to these family members, this context also recognised the norms that governed the operation of the family unit;

3. *School*—this includes the relationships a young person had with their peers and teachers, the social interactions that occurred at school, and the school and classroom policies;
4. *Public*—pertains to the immediate and extended aspects of the young people within their community, including social groups, governmental policy and practice, and the political and economic agendas; and
5. *Cyber*—relates to how young people used electronic communications.

Papatraianou et al. (2014) argue that the interaction between these five contexts is dynamic, reciprocal, and potentially multi-dimensional. Moreover, the amount of control that an individual has over the contexts also varies from relatively high for the personal level to relatively low for the public level. The risk factors that were proposed for cyberbullying included the speed of information transfer, the permanence of records, homophily of the social networks, the lack of a mechanism to confront perpetrators of cyberbullying, and increased access to technology. Conversely, positive relationships with family members, locus of control, high self-esteem, and a sense of meaning and purpose promoted resilience and together act as protective factors against cyberbullying. Further, positive peer relationships and school based mentoring programmes that promoted resilience are also likely to act as protective factors.

As with face-to-face bullying, peers may also be able to play an important intervening role in providing support for young people who experience cyberbullying. For example, Cowie and Colliety (2010) argue that peers can be used to monitor social network sites for instances of cyberbullying, provide support, and disclose incidences of cyberbullying. Peers can also be used as a mechanism to provide support to those involved in cyberbullying through offering email support. For example, Huston and Cowie (2007) trialled an email peer support scheme in an all boys' school in London. The scheme involved trained peer volunteers responding to queries about bullying via email. Young people at the school emailed a central address where teachers then anonymised the message and forwarded it on to the peer support volunteers who then responded via the teacher to the student. The system was designed so that the peer volunteers were unaware of who they were helping. Whilst the system was reported to be successful, one of the challenges of this multi-layered system was the time lag between the initial email being sent and the response back, although the aim was to respond to queries within 48 hours. However, Huston and Cowie advocated the email support system as a potential mechanism to offer peer support during cyberbullying because it provides individuals with the opportunity to seek support without preconceptions, personalities, or boundaries hindering the interactions.

In addition to acting as peer mentors, it has also been proposed that peers can act as tutors to teach younger children about the risks associated with digital technology use and cyberbullying. For example, Mustacchi (2009) described a peer-tutoring scheme that had been implemented in an American middle school. The scheme involved 8th grade students teaching 6th grade students about public safety using digital technology, including topics such as flaming, phishing, cyberbullying, cyber harassment, cyberbullying or harassment by proxy, and online grooming. The scheme has the advantage of developing the 6th grade students' knowledge of these areas and the 8th grade students' knowledge of netiquette whilst researching the topic areas. The scheme was positively reviewed by both groups of students.

Whilst a number of suggested interventions, recommendations, and guidelines have been outlined up until now in this chapter, there are a number of considerations that must be followed before interventions are implemented. For example, Marczak and Coyne (2010) generated a list of five recommendations that practitioners should consider when using interventions. First, it is necessary to raise awareness of cyberbullying and responsible technology use amongst young people, teachers, and parents. Second, existing school policies and practices should be updated to include cyberbullying with details included with regard to documenting instances of cyberbullying. Third, mechanisms for reporting cyberbullying should be simplified and could include student council, a task force, peer reports, anonymous reports, and direct contact with Internet service providers. Fourth, schools should promote positive technology use, including netiquette, e-safety, and digital literacy. Fifth, schools should evaluate the impact of the anti-cyberbullying strategies that they implement.

A recent review of the effectiveness of interventions to tackle cyberbullying argues that the majority of interventions designed to tackle cyberbullying lack scientific merit (Della Cioppa, O'Neil, & Craig, 2015). Specifically, Della Cioppa et al. argue that the interventions often lack the ability to engage multiple systematic levels, fail to modify the intervention for the specific school setting, and lack follow up measures to ensure that any positive benefits have been maintained over time. Further, out of the interventions that they reviewed, only seven yielded exclusively positive results. Della Cioppa et al. account for their findings concerning the relative success of cyberbullying interventions because the programmes often failed to examine whether their effects transcended from the school environment where they were delivered to the digital environment where cyberbullying occurs.

In addition to considering the effectiveness of interventions designed to tackle cyberbullying from the practitioners' and facilitators' point of view, it is also important to consider young people's perspectives. Understanding young people's perspectives with regard to what they think about the interventions is crucial because they are the ones that potentially experience both the interventions and cyberbullying. Paul, Smith, and Blumberg (2012) reported that 11- to 14-year-olds thought that the most appropriate intervention to tackle cyberbullying was an informal sanction undertaken by the school (25%), followed by a formal approach (13%), exclusion as a punishment (11%), and telling the young person's family what had happened (10%). The approaches that were least favoured by the young people were verbal warnings and providing pastoral support (6.5% each). Of course, these findings have implications for interventions that have been developed to offer support for those involved in cyberbullying. One factor that may be important is the role an individual plays within cyberbullying which may, in turn, impact on their perceptions of the most appropriate intervention. Further, Paul et al. report that many of the young people said that they did not like, or agree with, many of the sanctions that schools had developed and implemented in response to cyberbullying. However, when asked to provide their recommendations for tackling cyberbullying, the young people resorted to making suggestions of strategies that they had previously identified as something they disliked. Similarly, Davies, Randall, Ambrose, and Orand (2014) reported that frequently endorsed strategies for dealing with cyberbullying was to seek social support, ignore or block content, finding an expressive outlet, self-talk, and taking the bullies' perspective. However, the participants recognised that not all of these strategies were effective mechanisms for dealing with cyberbullying.

A similar line of research found that young people were more receptive to positive anti-cyberbullying messages, and these positive messages had the effects of leading to more positive anti-cyberbullying attitudes than negative messages (Alhabash et al., 2013). However, young people from Canada reported that they thought there was little that their school could do to tackle cyberbullying (Cassidy, Jackson, & Brown, 2009). Together, these findings reflect some of the challenges faced by schools with regard to cyberbullying interventions. Specifically, that is whilst they may be unpopular with young people, alternatives are not readily forthcoming. An alternative proposed by Olweus (2013) to address this issue is that rather than developing and implementing bespoke programmes designed to reduce cyberbullying, cyberbullying can be effectively reduced through participation in face-to-face bullying interventions. One such intervention which has been evaluated with regard to bullying and cyberbullying is philosophy for children (Tangen & Campbell, 2010). Philosophy for children involves developing a pluralistic community that is underpinned by collaboration and dialogue which together foster children's cognitive and social skills. Tangen and Campbell reported that the intervention reduced levels of bullying but not cyberbullying in 10- to 13-year-olds in the school where the intervention was delivered compared to the school that did not participate in the intervention. The authors argue that one of the challenges associated with anti-bullying interventions is that children do not always translate the skills that they have learnt into practice and that by enhancing children's ability to reflect may reduce bullying.

An alternative strategy proposed by Olweus (2013), whilst recognising the complexities of revealing the identity of a cyberbully, to reduce cyberbullying would be for schools to indentify a few perpetrators of cyberbullying and then communicate the details of these to fellow students in an anonymous manner. However, the anonymity of many perpetrators of cyberbullying also means that young people report that they fail to disclose experiences of cyberbullying to adults because they believe that adults will not be able to identify the perpetrators (Mishna et al., 2009). Further, the perception of anonymity and a lack of accountability online also predict engagement in cyberbullying (Barlett, 2015; Barlett & Gentile, 2012). Consequently, one way to reduce the impact of perceived anonymity online and the engagement in cyberbullying is to raise awareness that actions online are not anonymous as Internet Protocol addresses can be traced and histories on computers examined (Barlett, Gentile, & Chew, 2014). However, the issues around potential anonymity with regard to cyberbullying means that although it may be possible to identify which account a perpetrator used to target another individual, it is important to remember that someone else may have been using the account (Beale & Hall, 2007).

In summary, there are a number of interventions that have been developed to try to assist young people involved in cyberbullying, and a number of recommendations have been developed for parents and educational practitioners. Whilst there is some empirical evidence to support the effectiveness of these approaches, it is important to remember that as with other areas of cyberbullying, this is still an emerging area of research, and authors such as Della Cioppa et al. (2015) have called for more evidence-based research. Consequently, additional research is needed to fully investigate the effectiveness of the interventions in a range of samples, from a range of countries, and over a sustained period of time. It is also important to consider that as technology continues to evolve so too does cyberbullying; therefore, it is likely that the interventions must evolve to continue to be effective. The next section of the chapter will discuss the legal aspects associated with tackling cyberbullying.

6.2   THE LAW AND CYBERBULLYING

The legal position surrounding cyberbullying has been widely debated in terms of who should intervene when cyberbullying occurs. For example, Schultz (2014) argues that the current criminal law does not offer adequate protection of an individual's privacy rights in a digital context. Consequently, Schultz advocates the use of civil liability law or tort law as a mechanism for individuals who experience cyberbullying to seek justice.

Despite this debate, and lack of clarity surrounding the legal aspects of cyberbullying, there have been calls for specific laws to tackle cyberbullying (e.g., Stewart & Fritsch, 2011). Similarly, some practitioners have suggested tariffs under which individuals who engage in behaviours such as trolling can be prosecuted in the UK (e.g., Bishop, 2014). Butler, Kift, and Campbell (2009) argued that cyberbullying can be conceptualised as a criminal, tortuous, or vilifying behaviour and that whilst involving the police may be seen as extreme, it could facilitate the target to regain control over the situation that they experiencing. However, one of the challenges raised by Butler et al. was whether the perpetrator of cyberbullying could be held responsible for their actions. Reflecting on the possible challenges, Butler did suggest that prosecutions could be brought under laws associated with assault, threats, extortion, stalking, harassment, indecent conduct, torture, cyber stalking, and telecommunication offences. In addition to criminal proceedings, Butler et al. also advocates bringing charges under civil proceedings.

From a legal perspective, it has also been argued that schools have a responsibility for dealing with cyberbullying. For example, Hinduja and Patchin (2011) argue that schools in the USA should intervene in incidents of cyberbullying when: There is significant disruption to learning and the educational process, school resources are used in cyberbullying, and threats to others are made or civil rights are infringed. However, Hinduja and Patchin acknowledge that it is important that schools do have clear policies that outline responsible and acceptable behaviour and behaviour that constitutes cyberbullying and that is unacceptable. Of course, these policies would need to be continually updated as technology evolves.

Some states in America adopted legislation to deal with cyberbullying in 2009. For example, the California school district has the power to expel or suspend a student if they engage in cyberbullying (Darden, 2009). Darden also calls for schools to develop policies to protect staff and students from cyberbullying through ensuring suitable punishment for the actions of perpetrators of cyberbullying. The approach is advocated because technology enables young people to express themselves in a number of ways and some of which may be via impulsive acts. Therefore, Darden argues that schools need to implement punishments that will deter young people from engaging in cyberbullying, and these should also extend to cyberbullying acts that occur outside of school.

In addition to the suggested legislation around engaging in acts of cyberbullying, a number of other forms of legislation have been suggested. For example, Benzmiller (2013) called for a 'bad Samaritan law'. The purpose of this law would be to hold individuals who witness cyberbullying, but do not report it, as legally accountable for their actions as a mechanism to reduce the silence around cyberbullying. However, Benzmiller acknowledges that such a law could not become legislation until other laws were passed that addressed cyberbullying and issues around violating the target of cyberbullying's privacy. Further, Burton, Florell, and Wygant (2013) argue that young people may not intervene when they witness cyberbullying because of a diffusion of responsibility. Therefore, if a 'bad Samaritan law' was developed, it would have to cover all witnesses of cyberbullying to reduce potential diffusion of responsibility which may make such legislation unworkable.

Of course, it is important to acknowledge that whatever legislation is developed and implemented, it is imperative that young people are aware of the existence of such legislation and the associated consequences that it may bring. A relatively recent study conducted by Paul et al. (2012), with 11- to 14-year-olds in the UK, found that there was a significant gap between what the young people knew about the legality of cyberbullying and the legalisation at the time. Paul et al. argue that it is important that young people are aware of the potential legal consequences of cyberbullying because the age of criminal responsibility in the UK is ten.

A further example of violation of existing laws occurs in sexting. Sexting is the distribution of sexual images via small text message services or applications such as Instagram that allow images to be sent. Despite sexts (the images) often being sent in the context of romantic relationships, when relationships end or when the images circulated beyond the intended recipient, sexts can be a mechanism of cyberbullying. From a legal position, images of young people under 18 are classified as child pornography and when these images are circulated, this can be classified as distributing child pornography (Strassberg, Rullo, & Mackaronis, 2014). To tackle the challenge associated with sexting, McEllrath (2014) advocated a two tier approach with a distinction made between non-malicious juvenile sexting separated from malicious juvenile sexting. Further, it was advocated that the malicious form of juvenile sexting could be punished as a form of cyberbullying. A recent case in the UK, where a 14-year-old boy sent a naked image to a friend who then subsequently distributed to others highlights the complexity of the legal aspects of such behaviour (see http://www.bbc.co.uk/news/uk-34136388). As a result of the boy's behaviour, the police have recorded the incidence as a crime which could impact on his future.

Following on from the implications of children's lack of awareness over the legalities associated with cyberbullying, the developmental process may further impact on how laws associated with cyberbullying can be implemented. Specifically, Rodkin and Fischer (2012) question whether it is appropriate to develop laws concerning cyberbullying based on general versus specific intent. General intent may be appropriate for legislation concerning cyberbullying because of the possibility of the actions causing something other than distress. However, with regard to young people's engagement in cyberbullying, it may be more appropriate to adopt the principle of specific intent. The rationale for adopting specific intent, according to Rodkin and Fischer, is that younger children or children with limited experience of using digital technology may be less likely to appreciate and understand the consequences of their actions. Further, certain forms of cyberbullying may not fit the general intent principle. For example, messages sent about an individual who is not the intended recipient do not fit the general intention principle.

In summary, whilst there is some guidance with regard to the legal issues surrounding cyberbullying, it is clear that there is still ambiguity with regard to how these laws can be implemented and variation according to country. Perhaps one of the biggest challenges associated with the legal aspects of cyberbullying is the age of those involved. In particular, it has been debated with regard to whether intent can be identified and whether young people are cognitively aware of their actions.

6.3   PRACTICALITIES OF ADDRESSING CYBERBULLYING

A number of recommendations and suggestions have been made in this chapter with regard to how to tackle cyberbullying. However, it is important to contextualise these recommendations. First, technology and the functionality of technology continue to evolve, and, as such, it is likely that cyberbullying will also evolve; therefore, it is important that mechanisms to address cyberbullying also continue to evolve. Second, the roles that individuals can fulfil in cyberbullying are many and varied, including perpetrator, target, perpetrator/target, defender, and bystander (Barlińska, Szuster, & Winiewski, 2013). Consequently, researchers and practitioners need to develop strategies to support individuals who fulfil these various roles in the context of cyberbullying. Third, the timing of interventions should also be considered. For example, Couvillon and Ilieva (2011) advocate the use of an integrated whole school proactive interventions designed to foster digital citizenship rather than reactive interventions.

One of the biggest challenges surrounding anti-bullying interventions according to Ross (2013) is the cognitive and linguistic abilities of children. Ross argues that many interventions have limited success because many young people may not recognise that their actions constitute cyberbullying. Therefore, unless interventions help young people to identify and define their behaviour as cyberbullying, the interventions will not be successful. Further, children may lack the cognitive capabilities to process interventions that adopt a passive approach such as displaying posters, and they may also fail to internalise one off messages concerning cyberbullying. Another issue associated with children's developing cognitive skills is that they may not recognise the consequences of their actions and this may be particularly pertinent when they have little experience using technology. For example, Brydolf (2007) suggests that children may share inappropriate images without recognising that this may lead to unwanted attention from the wider audience.

In addition to the challenges associated with the children's cognitive and linguistic abilities, research has shown that the effectiveness of interventions designed to tackle bullying are influenced by the attitudes of those facilitating the interventions. Specifically, when students perceived teachers to be efficient in dealing with bullying, the students reported a reduction in bullying over time (Veenstra, Lindenberg, Huitsing, Sainio, & Salmivalli, 2014). Further, when the teachers were not perceived to be efficient by the students, and where positive attitudes towards bullying prevailed, these students engaged in higher levels of bullying. Teachers who have been regarded as 'effective' for dealing with cyberbullying are those who create a 'safe' space for young people to discuss with them the issues surrounding cyberbullying (Borgia & Myers, 2010). Similarly, if teachers model insensitive behaviour when dealing with the targets of bullying and make the target feel uncared for or blamed for their experiences, this may, in turn, promote and exacerbate the experiences of bullying (Yoon & Bauman, 2014).

Despite the many interventions, legal positions, and recommendations designed to address cyberbullying reviewed in this chapter, perhaps the most important mechanism to tackle cyberbullying is to develop an integrated approach (Vanderbosch, Beirens, D'Haese, Wegge, & Pabian, 2012). Vanderbosch et al. argue that in order to successfully tackle cyberbullying, young people, their parents, schools, police, and Internet service providers must all work together. Parents and schools should play an important role in the education of young people with regard to appropriate and responsible online behaviour and also monitor young people's online activities. Further, parents and schools must also be prepared to intervene in some incidences of cyberbullying; for example, by asking the perpetrator to delete material or by contacting Internet service providers to delete material. The police can also play an important role in addressing cyberbullying by educating young people, detecting and receiving complaints, and stopping potential crime. It is also recognised that the police often work with Internet service providers to identify those who engage in cyberbullying. However, Internet service providers are not always the content providers and this is important to acknowledge when cyberbullying occurs. Further, the police also rely on evidence that individuals are experiencing cyberbullying but this evidence is often deleted by targets so is not available to the police.

Given the recommendation that the police should be involved in tackling cyberbullying, it is important to consider their perception of the topic.

However, there is little research that has explored police officers' perceptions of cyberbullying. One such study was undertaken by Broll and Huey (2015) with Canadian police officers. Through a series of interviews, Broll and Huey identified that the police officers endorsed a preventative and educational approach as their preferred style to tackle cyberbullying. The officers believed that educating young people about the risks of using technology was more appropriate but also recognised that in some instances, legal action was appropriate but perceived that these cases extended beyond cyberbullying. In these cases, of what was perceived to be more series instances of cyberbullying, there was recognition that these had broken the law and, as such, required police intervention. However, 8 out of the 12 participants interviewed also endorsed the position that cyberbullying where young people were 'mean' to one another was not necessarily a crime.

The importance of developing appropriate policies and laws was underscored by a review of European Union practice (Genta, Brighi, & Guarini, 2009). Cyberbullying rates were found to be highest in the EU countries that did not have a global or systematic policy for dealing with cyberbullying. Therefore, according to Genta et al., shared national guidelines are vital for addressing the issue of cyberbullying.

In conclusion, this chapter has presented a range of interventions that have been developed by researchers and practitioners with the goal of reducing cyberbullying and assisting those who experience cyberbullying cope. The complex legal aspects associated with cyberbullying have also been outlined. As previously argued, it is important to consider the context with which interventions and laws are developed and implemented to ensure that they are effective in tackling cyberbullying. Further, it is also important to acknowledge that cyberbullying is an evolving phenomenon, and these changes present challenges for those trying to tackle cyberbullying.

REFERENCES

Ackers, M. J. (2012). Cyberbullying: Through the eyes of children and young people. *Educational Psychology in Practice: Theory, Research and Practice in Educational Psychology, 28,* 141–157.

Alhabash, S., McAlister, A. R., Hagerstrom, A., Taylor Quilliam, E., Rifon, N. J., & Richards, J. I. (2013). Between likes and shares: Effects of emotional appeal and virality on the persuasiveness of anticyberbullying messages on Facebook. *Cyberpsychology, Behavior, and Social Networking, 16,* 175–182.

Aricak, T., Siyahhan, S., Uzunhasanoglu, A., Saribeyoglu, S., Ciplak, S., Yilmaz, N., & Memmedov, C. (2008). Cyberbullying among Turkish adolescents. *CyberPsychology & Behavior, 11,* 253–261.

Barlett, C. P. (2015). Anonymously hurting others online: The effect of anonymity on cyberbullying frequency. *Psychology of Popular Media Culture, 4,* 70–79.

Barlett, C. P., & Gentile, D. A. (2012). Attacking others online: The formation of cyberbullying in late adolescence. *Psychology of Popular Media Culture, 1,* 123–135.

Barlett, C. P., Gentile, D. A., & Chew, C. (2014). Predicting cyberbullying from anonymity. *Psychology of Popular Media Culture.* Advanced online publication.

Barlińska, J., Szuster, A., & Winiewski, M. (2013). Cyberbullying among adolescent bystanders: Role of the communication medium, form of violence, and empathy. *Journal of Community & Applied Social Psychology, 23,* 37–51.

Beale, A. V., & Hall, K. R. (2007). Cyberbullying: What school administrators (and parents) can do. *Clearing House, 18,* 8–12.

Benzmiller, H. (2013). The cyber-Samaritans: Exploring criminal liability for the "innocent" bystanders of cyberbullying. *Northwestern University of Law Review, 107,* 927–962.

Bhat, C. S., Chang, S.-H., & Linscott, J. A. (2010). Addressing cyberbullying as a media literacy issue. *New Horizons in Education, 58,* 34–43.

Bishop, J. (2014). Digital teens and the 'antisocial network': Prevalence of troublesome online youth groups and internet trolling in Great Britain. *International Journal of E-Politics, 5,* 1–15.

Borgia, L. G., & Myers, J. J. (2010). Cyber safety and children's literature: A good match for creating classroom communities. *Illinois Reading Council Journal, 38,* 29–34.

Broll, R., & Huey, L. (2015). "Just being mean to somebody isn't a police matter": Police perspectives on policing cyberbullying. *Journal of School Violence, 14,* 155–176.

Bryant, A. (2009). *Beacon Street girls: Just kidding.* New York: Aladdin Paperbacks.

Brydolf, C. (2007). Minding MySpace: Balancing the benefits and risks of students' online social networks. *The Education Digest,* October, pp. 4–8.

Burton, K., Florell, D., & Wygant, D. B. (2013). The role of peer attachment and normative beliefs about aggression on traditional bullying and cyberbullying. *Psychology in the Schools, 50,* 103–115.

Butler, D., Kift, S., & Campbell, M. (2009). Cyber bullying in schools and the law: Is there an effective means of addressing the power imbalance? *eLaw Journal: Murdoch University Electronic Journal of Law, 16,* 84–114.

Campbell, M. (2011). School policy responses to the issue of cyber-bullying. *Journal of Catholic School Studies, 83,* 62–69.

Cassidy, W., Jackson, M., & Brown, K. N. (2009). Sticks and stones can break my bones, but how can pixels hurt me?: Students' experiences with cyber-bullying. *School Psychology International, 30*, 383–402.

Couvillon, M., & Ilieva, V. (2011). Recommended practices: A review of school-wide preventative programs and strategies on cyberbullying. *Preventing School Failure, 55*, 96–101.

Cowie, H., & Colliety, P. (2010). Cyberbullying: Sanctions or sensitivity? *Pastoral Care in Education, 28*, 261–268.

Davies, K., Randall, D. P., Ambrose, A., & Orand, M. (2014). 'I was bullied too': Stories of bullying and coping in an online community. *Information, Communication & Society, 18*, 357–375.

Darden, E. C. (2009, April). The cyber jungle. *American School Board Journal 196*, 54–56.

Dehue, F., Bolman, C., & Völlink, T. (2008). Cyberbullying: Youngsters' experiences and parental perception. *CyberPsychology & Behavior, 11*, 217–223.

Della Cioppa, V. D., O'Neil, A., & Craig, W. (2015). Learning from traditional bullying interventions: A review of research on cyberbullying and best practice. *Aggression and Violent Behavior.* doi:10.1016/j.avb.2015.05.009.

Diamanduros, T., Downs, E., & Jenkins, S. J. (2008). The role of school psychologists in the assessment, prevention, and intervention of cyberbullying. *Psychology in the Schools, 45*, 693–704.

Erdur-Baker, Ö. (2010). Cyberbullying and its correlation to traditional bullying, gender and frequent and risky usage on internet-mediated communication tools. *New Media & Society, 12*, 109–125.

Espinosa, P., & Clemente, M. (2013). Self-transcendence and self-oriented perspective as mediators between video game playing and aggressive behaviour in teenagers. *Journal of Community & Applied Social Psychology, 23*, 68–80.

Garaigordobil, M., & Martínez-Valderrey, V. (2015). Effects of cyberprogram 2.0 on "face-to-face" bullying, cyberbullying, and empathy. *Psicothema, 27*, 45–51.

Genta, M. L., Brighi, A., & Guarini, A. (2009). European project on bullying and cyberbullying granted by Daphne II programme. *Zeitschrift für Psychologie/ Journal of Psychology, 217*, 233.

Gradinger, P., Yanagida, T., Strohmeier, D., & Spiel, C. (2015). Prevention of cyberbullying and cyber victimization: Evaluation of the ViSC social competence programme. *Journal of School Violence, 14*, 87–110.

Hinduja, S., & Patchin, J. W. (2011). Cyberbullying: A review of the legal issues facing educators. *Preventing School Failure, 55*, 71–78.

Holfeld, B., & Grabe, M. (2012). Middle school students' perceptions of and responses to cyber bullying. *Journal of Educational Computing Research, 46*, 395–413.

Huston, N., & Cowie, H. (2007). Setting up an email peer support scheme. *Pastoral Care,* December, pp. 12–16.

Jackson, L. A., von Eye, A., Biocca, F. A., Barbatsis, G., Zhao, Y., & Fitzgerald, H. E. (2006). Does home internet use influence the academic performance of low-income children? *Developmental Psychology, 42*, 429–435.

Jacobs, N. C., Völlink, T., Dehue, F., & Lechner, L. (2014). Online pestkoppenstoppen: Systematic and theory-based development of a web-based tailored intervention for adolescent cyberbullying victims to combat and prevent cyberbullying. *BMC Public Health, 14*, 396.

Juvonen, J., & Gross, E. F. (2008). Extending the school grounds?—Bullying experiences in cyberspace. *Journal of School Health, 78*, 496–505.

Keith, S., & Martin, M. E. (2005). Cyber-bullying: Creating a culture of respect in a cyber world. *Reclaiming Children and Youth, 13*, 224–228.

Kite, S. L., Gable, R., & Filippelli, L. (2010). Assessing middle school students' knowledge of conduct and consequences and their behaviours regarding the use of social networking sites. *The Clearing House, 83*, 158–163.

Kueny, M. T., & Zirkel, P. A. (2012). An analysis of school anti-bullying laws in the United States. *Middle School Journal, 2012*, 22–31.

Lane, D. K. (2011). Taking the lead on cyberbullying: Why schools can and should protect students online. *Iowa Law Review, 96*, 1791–1811.

Law, D. M., Shapka, J. D., & Olson, B. F. (2010). To control or not control? Parenting behaviours and adolescent online aggression. *Computers in Human Behavior, 26*, 1651–1656.

Lazuras, L., Barkouskis, V., Ourda, D., & Tsorbatzoudis, H. (2013). A process model of cyberbullying in adolescence. *Computers in Human Behavior, 29*, 881–887.

Li, Q. (2006). Cyberbullying in schools: A research of gender differences. *School Psychology International, 27*, 157–170.

Machackova, H., Cerna, A., Sevcikova, A., Dedkova, L., & Daneback, K. (2013). Effectiveness of coping strategies for victims of cyberbullying. *Cyberpsychology: Journal of Psychosocial Research on Cyberspace, 7*, 3, article 5.

Marczak, M., & Coyne, I. (2010). Cyberbullying at school: Good practice and legal aspects in the United Kingdom. *Australian Journal of Guidance & Counselling, 20*, 182–193.

Mark, L., & Ratliffe, K. T. (2011). Cyber worlds: New playgrounds for bullying. *Computers in the Schools, 28*, 92–116.

McEllrath, R. (2014). Keeping up with technology: Why a flexible juvenile sexting statute is needed to prevent overly severe punishment in Washington State. *Washington Law Review, 89*, 1009–1033.

Merrell, K. W., Gueldner, B. A., Ross, S. W., & Isava, D. M. (2008). How effective are school bullying intervention programs? A meta-analysis of intervention research. *School Psychology Quarterly, 23*, 26–42.

Mishna, F., Saini, M., & Solomon, S. (2009). Ongoing and online: Children and youth's perceptions of cyber bullying. *Children and Youth Services Review, 31,* 1222–1228.

Mustacchi, J. (2009). R U safe? *Educational Leadership,* March, pp. 78–82.

Olweus, D. (2012). Cyberbullying: An overrated phenomenon? *European Journal of Developmental Psychology, 9,* 520–538.

Olweus, D. (2013). School bullying: Development and some important challenges. *Annual Review of Clinical Psychology, 9,* 751–780.

Pabian, S., & Vandebosch, H. (2014). Using the theory of planned behaviour to understand cyberbullying: The importance of beliefs for developing interventions. *European Journal of Developmental Psychology, 11,* 463–477.

Papatraianou, L. H., Levine, D., & West, D. (2014). Resilience in the face of cyberbullying: An ecological perspective on young people's experiences of online adversity. *Pastoral Care in Education: An International Journal of Personal, Social and Emotional Development, 32,* 264–283.

Paul, S., Smith, P. K., & Blumberg, H. H. (2012). Investigating legal aspects of cyberbullying. *Psicothema, 24,* 640–645.

Paullet, K., & Pinchot, J. (2014). Behind the screen where today's bully plays: Perceptions of college students on cyberbullying. *Journal of Information Systems Education, 25,* 63–69.

Pearce, N., Cross, D., Monks, H., Waters, S., & Falconer, S. (2011). Current evidence of best practice in whole-school bullying intervention and its potential to inform cyberbullying interventions. *Australian Journal of Guidance and Counselling, 21,* 1–21.

Raskauskas, J., & Stoltz, A. D. (2007). Involvement in traditional and electronic bullying among adolescents. *Developmental Psychology, 43,* 564–575.

Robinson, E. (2013). Parental involvement in preventing and responding to cyberbullying. *Family Matters, 92,* 68–76.

Rodkin, P. C., & Fischer, K. (2012). Cyberbullying from psychological and legal perspectives. *Missouri Law Review, 77,* 619–640.

Ross, P. (2013). A review of current bully etiology and why school bully interventions don't work. *Review of Higher Education and Self-Learning, 5,* 48–54.

Salmivalli, C. (2014). Participant roles in bullying: How can peer bystanders be utilized in interventions. *Theory Into Practice, 53,* 286–292.

Schultz, M. (2014). The responsible web: How tort law can save the internet. *Journal of European Tort Law, 5,* 182–204.

Sengupta, A., & Chaudhuri, A. (2011). Are social networking sites a source of online harassment for teens? Evidence from survey data. *Children and Youth Service Review, 33,* 284–290.

Simmons, K. D., & Bynum, Y. P. (2014). Cyberbullying: Six things administrators can do. *Education, 134,* 452–456.

Stauffer, S., Heath, M. A., Coyne, S. M., & Ferrin, S. (2012). High school teachers' perceptions of cyberbullying prevention and intervention strategies. *Psychology in the Schools, 49,* 353–367.

Stewart, D. M., & Fritsch, E. J. (2011). School and law enforcement efforts to combat cyberbullying. *Preventing School Failure, 55,* 79–87.

Strassberg, D. S., Rullo, J. E., & Mackaronis, J. E. (2014). The sending and receiving of sexually explicit cell phone photos ("sexting") while in high school: One college's students' retrospective reports. *Computers in Human Behavior, 41,* 177–183.

Tangen, D., & Campbell, M. (2010). Cyberbullying prevention: One primary school's approach. *Australian Journal of Guidance & Counselling, 20,* 225–234.

Thomas, S. P. (2006). From the editor—The phenomenon of cyberbullying. *Issues in Mental Health Nursing, 27,* 1015–1016.

Tokunaga, R. S. (2010). Following you home from school: A critical review and synthesis of research on cyberbullying victimization. *Computers in Human Behavior, 26,* 277–287.

Toshack, T., & Colmar, S. (2012). A cyberbullying intervention with primary-aged students. *Australian Journal of Guidance & Counselling, 22,* 268–278.

Vanderbosch, H., Beirens, L., D'Haese, W., Wegge, D., & Pabian, S. (2012). Police actions with regard to cyberbullying: The Belgian case. *Psicothema, 24,* 646–652.

Veenstra, R., Lindenberg, S., Huitsing, G., Sainio, M., & Salmivalli, C. (2014). The role of teachers in bullying: The relation between antibullying attitudes, efficacy, and efforts to reduce bullying. *Journal of Educational Psychology, 106,* 1135–1143.

Völlink, T., Bolman, C. A. W., Dehue, F., & Jacobs, N. C. L. (2013). Coping with cyberbullying: Differences between victims, bully-victims and children not involved in bullying. *Journal of Community & Applied Social Psychology, 23,* 7–24.

Whittaker, E., & Kowalski, R. M. (2015). Cyberbullying via social media. *Journal of School Violence, 14,* 11–29.

Wolfsberg, J. S. (2006). Student safety from cyberbullies, in chat rooms, and in instant messaging. *The Education Digest,* October, pp. 33–37.

Yoon, J., & Bauman, S. (2014). Teachers: A critical but overlooked component of bullying prevention and intervention. *Theory Into Practice, 53,* 308–314.

CHAPTER 7

Conclusions

Abstract Drawing together the arguments and research evidence presented throughout this book, this chapter will present seven areas of development for research into cyberbullying pertinent to all stakeholders. Specifically, the need for a common definition of cyberbullying, for agreement on the measures of cyberbullying, to establish accurate prevalence rates of cyberbullying, for longitudinal work to examine the consequences of cyberbullying, to develop robust and empirically validated interventions, and to recognise that technology in cyberbullying is evolving.

Keywords Cyberbullying • Definition • Future research

This final chapter will draw together the main arguments that have been presented elsewhere in this book. The chapter will suggest seven areas of development pertinent to all stakeholders involved in cyberbullying, including young people, educational practitioners, parents, researchers, and legal representatives. Through considering these areas of development, it will allow us to have not only a greater understanding of the area of cyberbullying but also will enable more accurate data to be collected.

7.1   THE NEED FOR A COMMON DEFINITION
OF CYBERBULLYING

As outlined in Chap. 2, and presented in Table 2.1, there are a number of definitions of cyberbullying that have been used by researchers in the area. Some of these definitions (e.g., Calvete, Orue, Estévez, Villardón, & Padilla, 2010) are developed from the principles of power imbalance, repetition, and intent associated with face-to-face bullying. Other researchers (e.g., Pieschl, Kuhlmann, & Prosch, 2015) have argued that cyberbullying is a distinct form of behaviour that requires further definition. What is clear from the existing literature is that, as Tokunaga (2010) proposed, the phrase cyberbullying has been used as somewhat of an 'umbrella' term to define a range of behaviours. Therefore, it is imperative that researchers develop a common definition of cyberbullying with a clear conceptualisation.

Developing a common definition of cyberbullying, as has happened for face-to-face bullying, would enable systematic comparisons to be made between studies because the same phenomenon has been examined. However, it is important that when the common definition of cyberbullying is agreed upon, it reflects the experiences of young people involved in cyberbullying. Working with young people to develop a definition of cyberbullying will ensure that the resulting definition accurately captures cyberbullying rather than some other form of aggression using digital technology. Further, it is also important to recognise that how young people interpret behaviour and actions depend on the context that they experience them in. For example, the same behaviour occurring between friends may be viewed as 'banter', but when repeated in a different situation, the behaviour may be considered to be an indicator of cyberbullying (Spenser & Betts, 2014).

7.2   THE NEED FOR AGREEMENT ON THE MEASURES
OF CYBERBULLYING

A related issue that closely follows on from how cyberbullying is defined is how cyberbullying is assessed. It is important that young people are aware of the definition and conceptualisation of cyberbullying that researchers are using to avoid them relying on their existing knowledge and taught definitions of cyberbullying (Pieschl et al., 2015). Although a number of measures of cyberbullying have been developed by researchers, these scales assess different behaviours across different media. Some of the measures use single items (e.g., Wachs, 2012) to assess cyberbullying, whereas others use multiple items (e.g., Menesini, Nocentini, & Calussi, 2011). Further, some measures assess young people's general experiences of cyberbullying (e.g., Aricak, 2009), whereas others focus on specific media (e.g., Mark & Ratliffe, 2011). The time frame that young people are asked to report on also varies from a relatively short (e.g., seven days, Lam, Cheng, & Liu, 2013) to longer periods (e.g., over the few months, Menesini et al., 2011) or unlimited time frames (e.g., Li, 2006). There are, of course, strengths and weaknesses with these different approaches. It is important to remember that the measure of cyberbullying used and the questions asked directly impact on the data that is gathered about young people's experiences of cyberbullying.

Ideally, once a common definition of cyberbullying has been agreed upon by researchers, scales or other measurement tools would be developed to ensure that all aspects of the definition are captured in the assessment of cyberbullying. By developing psychometrically robust measures that address all aspects of the definition of cyberbullying, it would overcome some of the limitations of existing measures. For example, some of the existing measures of cyberbullying do not manage to fully capture the power dynamic and repeated nature of cyberbullying both of which have been highlighted as critical facets.

7.3 THE NEED TO ESTABLISH ACCURATE PREVALENCE RATES OF CYBERBULLYING

As a consequence of establishing a common definition and psychometrically sound measures that assess cyberbullying, more accurate prevalence rates of cyberbullying can be determined. Currently, as evidenced in Table 4.1, there is a large variation in the reported prevalence rates of cyberbullying from the perspective of the target, perpetrator, and perpetrator/target. Smith (2004) advocates three reasons why establishing accurate prevalence rates of face-to-face bullying is vital: (1) to raise awareness of cyberbullying, (2) to enable comparisons between samples and populations, and (3) to draw inferences of the relative success of anti-bullying interventions. Of course, the same logic can be applied to cyberbullying to illustrate why it is important to establish accurate prevalence rates.

Although some of this variation in the reported prevalence of cyber-bullying, in the existing literature and documented in Table 4.1, can be accounted for because of differences relating to the sample studied, including factors such as age, sex, and country, some of this variation is likely to reside in the definition, conceptualisation, and measurement of cyberbullying. Therefore, when researchers have a shared understanding of what constitutes cyberbullying, this will go some way to address some of the issues associated with the reported prevalence rates of cyberbully-ing. Another challenge of assessing young people's experiences of cyber-bullying that researchers must find a way to take into consideration, when they are collecting data, is that young people often under-report their experiences of cyberbullying because they fear that their access to technol-ogy will be removed (Mishna, Saini, & Solomon, 2009; Thomas, 2006). Further, for some young people, the fear of missing out (Przybylski, Murayama, DeHaan, & Gladwell, 2013) is greater than the consequences of their experiences of cyberbullying. Consequently, in future, researchers and practitioners must take steps to ensure that the reports of cyberbully-ing are accurate, either by using technology driven mechanisms to capture experiences or experience sampling as advocated by Runions (2013).

7.4   The Need for Longitudinal Work to Examine the Consequences of Cyberbullying

As discussed in Chap. 5, there is a wealth of studies that have examined the concurrent associations between involvement in cyberbullying and some of the consequences of this involvement. The research has reported a range of associations, including psychosocial adjustment, general adjust-ment, and further involvement in cyberbullying for both the perpetra-tors and the targets of cyberbullying. The majority of studies that have been conducted to date have focused on concurrent associations which mean that it is difficult to infer causality in these relationships. These stud-ies have also tended to focus on either the targets of cyberbullying (e.g., Imamura et al., 2009) or the perpetrators (e.g., Campbell, Slee, Spears, Butler, & Kift, 2013), although it is important to acknowledge that young people who fulfil other roles in the cyberbullying episode such as perpetra-tor/target or observer may also experience consequences. Some research-ers have undertaken longitudinal studies examining the consequences of involvement in cyberbullying (e.g., Gámez-Guadix, Gini, & Calvete, 2015). However, these studies have tended to be over a limited duration and, whilst one explanation for this is likely to be the relative 'newness' of cyberbullying, there is a need to consider the longer-term effects.

By understanding the longer-term effects and consequences of involvement in cyberbullying, it will enable researchers to understand the seriousness of cyberbullying. Additionally, research is needed that examines the mediators in the relationship between cyberbullying involvement and the consequences, because as noted in Chap. 5, not all individuals who are involved in cyberbullying experience consequences. One likely reason for this is that there are factors that serve to protect or exacerbate the consequences of being involved in cyberbullying. Understanding the role of these factors could also help to inform interventions designed to tackle cyberbullying.

7.5   The Need to Develop Robust and Empirically Validated Interventions

In Chap. 6, a number of interventions that have been developed to tackle cyberbullying were reviewed. Guidance for supporting young people who experience cyberbullying has also been developed for educational practitioners and parents. Common to all of these interventions is the need to develop young people's skills for dealing with cyberbullying and also their knowledge of appropriate behaviour when using technology. Whilst some of the interventions appear to deliver promising results for those involved in cyberbullying, some studies have reported that the effectiveness of the interventions is modest at best. There is also the need for more evidence based research concerning the effectiveness of anti-cyberbullying interventions as Della Cioppa, O'Neil, and Craig (2015) advocate. Further, it is important that as interventions are developed, they reflect the various roles young people fulfil in cyberbullying (Barlińska, Szuster, & Winiewski, 2013). However, as Vanderbosch, Beirens, D'Haese, Wegge, and Pabian (2012) argue, perhaps the most effective way to tackle cyberbullying is through developing an integrated approach that involves young people, their parents, schools, the police, and Internet service providers.

7.6   The Need to Clarify the Legal Status of Cyberbullying

Closely aligned to the issues surrounding tackling cyberbullying, from an intervention perspective, is the ambiguity over who is responsible for addressing cyberbullying. Compared to face-to-face bullying, as

Tokunaga (2010) notes, there is a lack of consensus with regard to who regulates cyberbullying. One reason for this is that, unlike face-to-face bullying, cyberbullying can occur at any time and often happens outside of school. Whilst some argue that it is the school's responsibility to deal with behaviour that impacts on the school environment (e.g., Campbell, 2011), the right for freedom of speech complicates the situation (Brydolf, 2007).

Currently there is an ongoing debate with regard to the legal status of cyberbullying and whether current legalisation goes far enough to protect users of technology (e.g., Schultz, 2014). Regardless of how the law evolves, with regard to cyberbullying, it is important that young people are aware of the existence of legislation. There is evidence that young people are not aware of the current legislation in the UK relating to cyberbullying (Paul, Smith, & Blumberg, 2012). Consequently, if legislation is tightened to address cyberbullying, it is important that young people receive education with regard to what the legal status of cyberbullying is, so that they do not unintentionally break the law.

7.7   The Need to Recognise That Technology and Cyberbullying is Evolving

Finally, pertinent to all of areas that have been presented in this chapter, it is important that all stakeholders recognise that technology and cyberbullying are both continuing to evolve. For example, as new forms of technology become available so to do new mechanisms to cyberbully. This is perhaps exemplified best by the changing capabilities of mobile telephones: Early models of mobile telephones were used to cyberbully via text messages but as smart mobile telephones have been developed so to have the opportunities to cyberbully. Therefore, researchers need to be mindful that cyberbullying is likely to continue to evolve with technology and, as such, it is important that definitions, conceptualisations, and measurement tools reflect these changes. In addition to the evolution of the technology, it is also likely that young people's preferences for particular types of technology and media will change similar to the move from MySpace to Facebook by Australian youth as documented by (Boyd, 2011).

In conclusion, this chapter has argued that there are seven aspects of cyberbullying that need to be addressed. Perhaps the most important of these is to agree a common definition of cyberbullying that reflects young people's experiences. This is of upmost importance because once a common definition has been agreed upon, then robust tools to assess cyberbullying can be developed. Once these robust measures have been developed and validated, it will give us a more accurate understanding of young people's experiences of cyberbullying and the consequences associated with involvement in cyberbullying which will enable appropriate interventions to be developed and implemented. However, it is important to recognise that cyberbullying is likely to continue to evolve with technology, and consequently, it is important that the definitions, assessment tools, and interventions are future-proofed.

REFERENCES

Aricak, O. T. (2009). Psychiatric symptomatology as a predictor of cyberbullying among university students. *Eurasian Journal of Educational Research, 34*, 167–184.

Barlińska, J., Szuster, A., & Winiewski, M. (2013). Cyberbullying among adolescent bystanders: Role of the communication medium, form of violence, and empathy. *Journal of Community & Applied Social Psychology, 23*, 37–51.

Boyd, D. (2011). White flight in networked publics? How race and class shaped American teen engagement with MySpace and Facebook. In L. Nakamura & P. A. Chow-White (Eds.), *Race after the internet* (pp. 203–222). New York: Routledge.

Brydolf, C. (2007). Minding MySpace: Balancing the benefits and risks of students' online social networks. *The Education Digest*, October, pp. 4–8.

Calvete, E., Orue, I., Estévez, A., Villardón, L., & Padilla, P. (2010). Cyberbullying in adolescents: Modalities and aggressors' profile. *Computers in Human Behavior, 26*, 1128–1135.

Campbell, M. (2011). School policy responses to the issue of cyber-bullying. *Journal of Catholic School Studies, 83*, 62–69.

Campbell, M. A., Slee, P. T., Spears, B., Butler, S., & Kift, S. (2013). Do cyberbullies suffer too? Cyberbullies' perceptions of the harm they cause to others and to their own mental health. *School Psychology International, 34*, 613–629.

Della Cioppa, V. D., O'Neil, A., & Craig, W. (2015). Learning from traditional bullying interventions: A review of research on cyberbullying and best practice. *Aggression and Violent Behavior*. doi:10.1016/j.avb.2015.05.009.

Gámez-Guadix, M., Gini, G., & Calvete, E. (2015). Stability of cyberbuyllying victimization among adolescents: Prevalence and association with bully-victim status and psychosocial adjustment. *Computers in Human Behavior, 53,* 140–148.

Imamura, A., Nishida, A., Nakazawa, N., Shimodera, S., Tanaka, G., Kinoshita, H., ... & Okazaki, Y. (2009). Effects of cellular phone email use on the mental health of junior high school students in Japan. *Psychiatry and Clinical Neurosciences, 63,* 703.

Lam, L. T., Cheng, Z., & Liu, X. (2013). Violent online games exposure and cyberbullying/victimization among adolescents. *Cyberpsychology, Behavior, and Social Networking, 16,* 159–164.

Li, Q. (2006). Cyberbullying in schools: A research of gender differences. *School Psychology International, 27,* 157–170.

Mark, L., & Ratliffe, K. T. (2011). Cyber worlds: New playgrounds for bullying. *Computers in the Schools, 28,* 92–116.

Menesini, E., Nocentini, A., & Calussi, P. (2011). The measurement of cyberbullying: Dimensional structure and relative item severity and discrimination. *Cyberpsychology, Behavior, and Social Networking, 14,* 267–274.

Mishna, F., Saini, M., & Solomon, S. (2009). Ongoing and online: Children and youth's perceptions of cyber bullying. *Children and Youth Services Review, 31,* 1222–1228.

Paul, S., Smith, P. K., & Blumberg, H. H. (2012). Investigating legal aspects of cyberbullying. *Psicothema, 24,* 640–645.

Pieschl, S., Kuhlmann, C., & Prosch, T. (2015). Beware of publicity! Perceived distress of negative cyber incidents and implications for defining cyberbullying. *Journal of School Violence, 14,* 111–132.

Przybylski, A. K., Murayama, K., DeHaan, C. R., & Gladwell, V. (2013). Motivational, emotional, and behavioral correlates of fear of missing out. *Computers in Human Behavior, 29,* 1841–1848.

Runions, K. C. (2013). Toward a conceptual model of motive and self-control in cyber-aggression: Rage, revenge, reward, and recreation. *Journal of Youth and Adolescence, 42,* 99–136.

Schultz, M. (2014). The responsible web: How tort law can save the internet. *Journal of European Tort Law, 5,* 182–204.

Smith, P. K. (2004). Bullying: Recent developments. *Child and Adolescent Mental Health, 9,* 98–103.

Spenser, K. A., & Betts, L. R. (2014, May). "People think it's a harmless joke when really it could be hurting someone": Young people's experiences of cyber bullying. Poster presented at the *British Psychological Society Annual Conference,* International Convention Centre, Birmingham.

Thomas, S. P. (2006). From the editor—The phenomenon of cyberbullying. *Issues in Mental Health Nursing, 27,* 1015–1016.

Tokunaga, R. S. (2010). Following you home from school: A critical review and synthesis of research on cyberbullying victimization. *Computers in Human Behavior, 26,* 277–287.

Vanderbosch, H., Beirens, L., D'Haese, W., Wegge, D., & Pabian, S. (2012). Police actions with regard to cyberbullying: The Belgian case. *Psicothema, 24,* 646–652.

Wachs, S. (2012). Moral disengagement and emotional and social difficulties in bullying and cyberbullying: Differences by participant role. *Emotional and Behavioural Difficulties, 17,* 347–360.

INDEX

© The Editor(s) (if applicable) and The Author(s) 2016   143
L.R. Betts, *Cyberbullying*, DOI 10.1057/978-1-137-50009-0